The Workplace
PERSONAL SKILLS FOR SUCCESS

Dr. Joe Pace

McGraw Hill

Boston   Burr Ridge, IL   Dubuque, IA   Madison, WI   New York   San Francisco   St. Louis
Bangkok   Bogotá   Caracas   Kuala Lumpur   Lisbon   London   Madrid   Mexico City
Milan   Montreal   New Delhi   Santiago   Seoul   Singapore   Sydney   Taipei   Toronto

The McGraw-Hill Companies

Higher Education

*A division of the **McGraw-Hill** Companies*

THE PROFESSIONAL DEVELOPMENT SERIES: BOOK THREE: THE WORKPLACE: PERSONAL SKILLS FOR SUCCESS
Published by McGraw-Hill, a business unit of The McGraw-Hill Companies, Inc., 1221 Avenue of the Americas, New York, NY, 10020.
Copyright © 2006 by The McGraw-Hill Companies, Inc. All rights reserved. No part of this publication may be reproduced or
distributed in any form or by any means, or stored in a database or retrieval system, without the prior written consent of The McGraw-
Hill Companies, Inc., including, but not limited to, in any network or other electronic storage or transmission, or broadcast for distance
learning.

Some ancillaries, including electronic and print components, may not be available to customers outside the United States.

This book is printed on acid-free paper.

2 3 4 5 6 7 8 9 0 CUS/CUS 0 9 8 7 6 5

ISBN   0-07-829830-X

Publisher: *Beth Mejia*
Executive editor: *David S. Patterson*
Developmental editor: *Anne Sachs*
Senior marketing manager: *Leslie Oberhuber*
Senior media producer: *Todd Vaccaro*
Project manager: *Jean R. Starr*
Production supervisor: *Janean A. Utley*
Associate designer: *Srdjan Savanovic*
Media project manager: *Todd Vaccaro*
Photo research coordinator: *Natalia C. Peschiera*
Art editor: *Ayelet Arbel*
Photo researcher: *Natalia C. Peschiera*
Art director: *Jeanne Schreiber*
Cover design: *Srdj Savanovic*
Interior design: *Kiera Pohl*
Typeface: *9.5/12 Palatino*
Compositor: *Carlisle Communications, Ltd.*
Printer: *Von Hoffmann Custom*

www.mhhe.com

Contents

As a psychologist and former college president involved in higher education for over 36 years, I often have been asked what skills most directly contribute to career success.

The questioner generally expects me to talk about job skills. Thirty years ago, it would have been typing. Today, it might be familiarity with common workplace software.

But the fact is that most employers don't care how fast you type or how well you align columns on a spreadsheet.

What Do Employers Want?

In a recent survey,* business owners and corporate executives in the United States were asked to rate what they valued most in a new employee:

- Dependability—35%
- Honesty—27%
- Good attitude—19%
- Competence—19%

What does this tell us? It says, simply, that 81 percent of corporations in the United States rate the personal qualities of dependability, honesty, and attitude—what I call *professionalism*—above any skills-based competencies.

The Need for *Professionalism*

Does it make sense that employers value professionalism over what we generally think of as job-related skills? Certainly. All jobs and businesses are different. Even companies manufacturing similar products in the same city will have their own unique procedures and policies. Working for one does not mean you can easily transition into working for another. Employers know this. They know that they will have to train you in the skills necessary for your job and they are willing to do this. What employers want from you are the internal qualities that make you trainable.

Employers want you to be reliable; they want you to be hardworking; and they want you to be ethical. In a word, employers look for the qualities that make a person *professional*.

Padgett Business Services, quarterly survey of service and retail clients.

Why *The Professional Development Series?*

The sad fact is that most colleges and schools spend an overwhelming majority of the time and energy developing hard skills while ignoring the personal qualities of character and dependability that actually get people hired. The good news is that—like typing or programming—professionalism can be taught.

My aim in developing this *Professional Development Series* has been to teach the personal skills that lead to job and career success. The *Series* is based on both my own research on career success and my experience as a lecturer, college president, and mentor. The material I present in the *Series* is the same material I have used to guide thousands of students and to train hundreds of instructors across North America. The goal for teachers who use the *Series* is to help turn out graduates ready to meet the challenges of the fast-paced professional world. The goal for students learning with the *Series* is to succeed in their chosen careers and, more importantly, to succeed in life.

The Books in *The Professional Development Series*

The Professional Development Series is easy to read and user-friendly. The books are brief, because you are busy. The books are practical, because you need specific guidance, not vague assurances. Each book and every chapter use a consistent organization of text and features to structure the material.

Book 1: The Workplace: Today and Tomorrow

Book 1 is an orientation to the world of work. In it, you will consider the occupations that are most likely to have job openings in the coming years, how to prepare yourself to fill these openings, and what the workplace environment is like in the twenty-first century. Professional business protocol, professional presence, and a customer-first attitude also are explored and discussed.

Book 2: The Workplace: Interpersonal Strengths and Leadership

Professional success in the twenty-first century demands that people work together to achieve their goals. Book 2: *Interpersonal Strengths and Leadership* explores and develops the skills that make a person a good teammate and a good leader. Developing a standard of excellence and pride in your work along with understanding ethics, trust, and respect also is covered. Thinking strategically and modeling leadership techniques are addressed as well.

Book 3: The Workplace: Personal Skills for Success

Time management and stress management come to mind when we talk about *Personal Skills for Success* and in Book 3, you will develop and practice these skills. You also will be encouraged to think about who you are and what you believe and to use what you learn to establish goals for the future and to develop a plan to achieve those goals. Communicating and presenting ideas and concepts, as well as thinking critically and creatively, also are covered.

Book 4: The Workplace: Chart Your Career

One day you leave school and you have a job; 20 years later you look back and realize that you have a career. How can you make sure that thecareer you have is fulfilling and rewarding? How can you avoid or overcome the inevitable missteps—taking the wrong job, for example— and get your career back on track? Book 4 offers guidance on planning a career and, more importantly, on developing, changing, and maintaining it.

Features of Each Book in *The Professional Development Series*

Every chapter of each book has a consistent format, clearly organizing the material to help you learn.

Beginning Each Chapter **What Will You Do?** The entire plan for the chapter is set out in What Will You Do? Each section within the chapter is called out with a one-sentence summary describing the content.

Why Do You Need to Know This? The information in each chapter is there for a reason. Why Do You Need to Know This? explains how the material will be useful in finding a job, building a rewarding career, or succeeding in life.

Set the Pace Before beginning a chapter, it is important to determine what you already know about the topic. Set the Pace asks you to think about your own experiences with the subject.

Objectives These are your goals for the chapter. When you have done the reading and the work for each chapter, you should have learned about and practiced each of the bulleted skills. These Objectives will be revisited in the Chapter Summary.

Beginning Each Section **Reading and Study Tip** Each tip presents a helpful suggestion to aid your retention of the material in the section.

In Each Section **Quotations** These thoughts offer inspiration, context, and perspective from important and influential people in all walks of life.

Vocabulary Important terms are called out in the margins and defined.

New Attitudes/New Opportunities These profiles present real people giving voice to their real-world goals, concerns, and experiences.

Pace Points These are techniques and advice that I have found useful from my own work experience.

Judgment Call These real-world scenarios call on you to interpret and act on the information in the section. Check your answers online at www.mhhe.com/pace.

Dr. Joe Pace These are quotations from my workshops that, over time, my students have found the most meaningful.

Ending Each Section **Quick Recap** Here is a summary to help you review the section material, check yourself with short review questions, and check your answers online at www.mhhe.com/pace.

Chapter Review and Activities **Chapter Summary** The chapter's Objectives reappear here with a review of what you should know about each section and about each objective.

Business Vocabulary All the vocabulary terms from the chapter are listed with the page number where they can be found within the chapter. Double-check to make sure you know what each word means and how it is used.

Key Concept Review Short-answer questions in the Key Concept Review will help you remember the material from each section.

Online Project Go online to learn more about what you have learned in the chapter.

Step Up the Pace These real-world scenarios help you think about applying what you have learned in the chapter to your own life, job, and career.

Business Skills Brush-Up This activity gives you the chance to practice important business skills such as critical reading and effective writing.

Support for *The Professional Development Series*

The books of the *Series* are supported by

Professional Development Series **Web site (www.mhhe.com/pace)** On the Web site, students can find answers to questions posed in the text, additional chapter review materials, and topics for additional reading and study. Instructors also can access sample syllabi, suggested test questions, and tips for teaching.

Study Smart **Study Skills Tutorial** From time management to taking notes, *Study Smart* is an excellent way to practice your skills. *Study Smart* was developed by Andrea Bonner and Mieke Schipper of Sir Sanford Fleming College and is available on CD-ROM (0–07–245515–2). This innovative study skills tutorial teaches students essential note-taking methods, test-taking strategies, and time management secrets. *Study Smart* is free when packaged with the books of *The Professional Development Series.*

BusinessWeek **Online** Interested instructors can offer their students 15 weeks of access to *BusinessWeek* Online by requesting that a password card be packaged with the books of *The Professional Development Series.* For further information call 1–800–338–3987 or speak to your McGraw-Hill Sales Representative.

Instructor's Resource **CD-ROM** This is a thorough guide to planning, organizing, and administering courses using *The Professional Development Series.* The CD includes sample syllabi, model assessments, and test questions, and teaching tips for each section in every chapter of all four books.

About the Author

For over 36 years, Dr. Joe Pace has been a nationally recognized speaker, author, and educator. A psychologist and former college president, Dr. Pace currently serves as the managing partner of the Education Initiative for The Pacific Institute.

Dr. Pace is creator of the *Success Strategies for Effective Colleges and Schools* program implemented worldwide in over 200 colleges and schools. He has served as commissioner of the Accrediting Council of Independent Colleges and Schools (ACICS) in Washington, D.C.; on the board of directors of The Association of Independent Colleges and Schools, now known as the CCA (Career College Association); and as president of the Florida Association of Postsecondary Schools and Colleges.

A popular keynote speaker at conferences and conventions, Dr. Pace also has conducted a variety of seminars and workshops throughout North America on such topics as school management, faculty development, student retention, psychology, and motivation. Thousands of college-level students have benefited from his expertise in the areas of psychology, personal development, and business administration.

Dr. Pace is known for his warmth, enthusiasm, humor, and "intelligent heart." His audiences enjoy his genuine spirit and heartwarming stories. Because of his loving and caring nature, Dr. Pace is able to help people to succeed in their chosen careers, but more importantly, to succeed in life.

Acknowledgments

The energy to develop this series has come from my family: my wife Sharon, my daughters Tami and Tiffany, my son-in-law John, and my grandkids Nicholas, Jessica, Dylan, and Jonathan. Their love and support get me up in the morning, inspire my work, and excite me about tomorrow.

Thanks also to Shawn Knieriem, my director of operations, for her assistance and support with this project.

My special thanks to the Advisory Board and Review Panel for their excellent suggestions, tips, techniques, and wisdom, as well as for their time and effort in attending various meetings. I have considered them friends and colleagues for many years and it was an honor to work with them on this project.

Advisory Board In October of 2002, a group of educators came together to chart the course for the project that would become *The Professional Development Series.* Their insights and vision guided me.

Teresa Beatty, ECPI

Gary Carlson, ITT Educational Services

Jerry Gallentine, National American University

Gery Hochanadel, Keiser College

Jim Howard, Sanford Brown Colleges

Ken Konesco, Indiana Business Colleges

Review Panel Once the Board provided the goal, the Review Panel undertook to develop the project. Their sage advice influenced every page of *The Professional Development Series.*

Steve Calabro, Southwest Florida College

JoAnna Downey, Corinthian Colleges

Barb Gillespie, Cuyamaca College

Lynn Judy, Carteret Community College

Ken Konesco, Indiana Business Colleges

Ada Malcioln, International Institute of the Americas

Dena Montiel, Santa Ana School of Continuing Education

Peggy Patlan, Fox College

Sharon Roseman, Computer Career Center

Peggy Schlechter, National American University

The Workplace

Establish Values, Goals, and Attitude

What Will You Do?

1.1 Assessing What You Want To get what you want out of your career—and out of life—determine exactly what you do want. This section guides you in taking into account your value system and personal goals as well as your professional goals, then setting priorities.

1.2 Assessing Your Strengths Strengths include interests and aptitudes, as well as skills. Learn how to determine current and future strengths.

1.3 Setting Your Personal Goals Learn how personal goals are essential to professional success. This section guides you in setting and reaching your personal goals.

1.4 Setting Your Professional Goals Read about the difference between career and job goals. This section guides you in setting and reaching your professional goals.

1.5 Setting Your Attitude Everyone fails. Your attitude and reactions to the experience can make all the difference in where you go from there. Use this section to help change an attitude.

Why It's Important

If you want to get somewhere, it helps to know where you want to go. You need a destination, a goal—and you need to know how to get there. If you don't know where you're going, you will wander. You may waste a lot of time, and you may end up where you'd rather not be.

This applies to a road trip as well as to your profession and your life. As far as your profession and your life go, some of the biggest decisions you'll ever make concern your goals: where you want to go and how you're going to get there. It's never too soon to make those decisions, and it's never wrong to change them. This chapter will help you get started in the process of deciding what you want, what you're good at, where you want to go, and how you're going to get there.

Chapter Objectives

After completing this chapter, you will be able to

- Recognize what you want and set benchmarks for getting there.

- Assess your strengths, skills, and aptitudes and orient them to your goals.

- Set personal goals and determine the steps you must take to reach them.

- Set professional goals and determine the steps you must take to reach them.

- Set your attitude on positive, take rejection and failure for what they're worth, and grow from your experiences.

Set the *Pace*

Toot Your Own Horn Think about what you've already accomplished in your life. Make a list of your highest achievements in (a) school, (b) sports or a hobby, (c) making money, (d) financial responsibilities (such as a mortgage), and (e) making yourself proud.

- How long did you work for each of these accomplishments?
- Who set these goals—you or someone else?
- Which of these accomplishments has set you up for a bigger accomplishment?

Activity Write a one-page autobiography about what you've accomplished in your life, starting with the earliest steps that led up to those accomplishments. Then write another page about how you can build on those accomplishments to reach even higher goals. In a class discussion, talk about why you'd like to reach those new goals.

Assessing What You Want

What's important to you? What do you want to do with your life? How are you going to match the ideals of your life and the responsibilities of your career? How much can you accomplish? What do you have to do to get where you want to go? *These are not easy questions.* In fact, you'll probably spend the rest of your life thinking about them and adjusting your answers from a few years earlier.

What Do You Want?   The first step toward getting what you want is knowing what you want. That's a complicated question with a lot of complicated answers. In this section, you'll apply a critical eye to your many interests and think hard about what you'd like to get out of life.

> *To me, success means effectiveness in the world, that I am able to carry my ideas and values into the world—that I am able to change it in positive ways.*
>
> *Maxine Hong Kingston*
> *Contemporary American Author*

values the basic beliefs that are important to you, the ones that guide your choices and tell you what is right or wrong

What Do You Want?

The world has no shortage of options. In fact, you have more options for your life than any one life can possibly accomplish. You can get married or stay single. You can stay in school until you get a Ph.D., or you can drop out now and never go back. You can work in a bank, a fire department, or a soup kitchen. You can work hard to grab every possible dollar, or you can live on a shoestring and follow a career that offers other kinds of satisfaction.

But the options aren't infinite. Some may not interest you at all. Some are beyond your ability. Some might be interesting *and* possible, but you can't do them all. You can't be a professional baseball player *and* an astronaut *and* mayor of your town . . . at least not all at the same time.

Your Values: What's Important to You

The decisions you make about how you want to live and what you want to do for a living depend fundamentally on your **values.** Your values are the basic beliefs that are important to you, the ones that guide your choices and tell you what is right or wrong for you. Everybody has his or her own set of values. Here are just a few of the many values that people have:

- Having a lot of free time
- Being productive
- Being helpful
- Being respected as a man or woman
- Being respected as a citizen
- Being attractive
- Being loved

- Having a lot of money
- Giving your family a better life
- Health
- Physical strength
- Honesty
- Knowledge
- Power

- Making the world a better place
- God and the morality of a religion
- Maximizing pleasure
- Financial security
- Working with other people
- Working alone

- Being in charge
- Living with nature
- Enjoying culture
- Perpetual learning
- Taking life easy
- Being a good parent

Your values are, by definition, important to you. You should take the time to think about them and write them down. This is something you can do periodically for the rest of your life. The total of all your values and the way they work together is your personal **value system.** By understanding your own value system, you will be better able to set realistic and satisfying goals.

value system the total of all your values and the way they work together

Two Value Systems

Noreen and Aaron are both about to graduate from Centerville Vocational-Technical School. They've both concentrated on communication, but their value systems are quite different, and they're likely to set different goals and pursue different careers.

Noreen's Values	Aaron's Values
Being honest	Being honest
Being productive	Being productive
Being competitive and winning	Avoiding competition
Being attractive	Helping others
Being in charge	Being independent
Being respected for her accomplishments	Being respected for his accomplishments
Being respected for her possessions	Being respected for his knowledge
Being with important people	Spending time with family

Neither of these value systems is better than the other; they are simply different. If Noreen and Aaron are going to be happy in their lives, they will probably have to pursue different goals.

Internet Quest

Reaching a Goal

Go online to find five sites that are related to your personal goals. They could be sites featuring a car you want to buy or the school you want your child to attend. Find an image on each site and print it. Paste the images together on a separate sheet of paper to make a collage of your goals. Keep the collage in your career portfolio to remind yourself why you are working.

Linking Values and Goals

Goals are end results. Your values tell you where to aim your efforts. They determine your goals. Goals let you put your values into action. As long as your values are driving you toward your goals, you can find as much satisfaction in pursuing those goals as you do in reaching them.

goals the ultimate aim of your efforts

What Are Your Benchmark Goals?

benchmark goals points or standards from which you can measure or locate other things; in terms of goals, the important goals that are unlikely to change

Benchmarks are points or standards from which you can measure or locate other things. When you think about your goals, benchmarks are indispensable: they are the goals that stand no matter what, the ones that all other goals must fit around. For example, if spending a lot of time with your family is a benchmark, then you don't need to consider career goals that would have you traveling constantly. If a good salary is of benchmark importance, your goals might lead toward a career in business or information technology rather than social work or retail sales.

What are your benchmark goals—the aspects of your life and career that are of absolute importance? Look at Aaron's and Noreen's benchmarks as examples. Note how they fit in with their respective values.

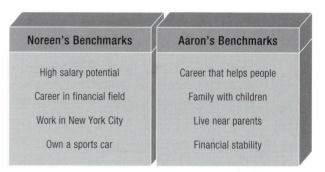

Noreen's Benchmarks	Aaron's Benchmarks
High salary potential	Career that helps people
Career in financial field	Family with children
Work in New York City	Live near parents
Own a sports car	Financial stability

Thinking About Benchmark Goals

Benchmarks are worth a lot of thought. You'll be making a lot of other decisions based on your benchmarks. You can change them, of course, but that may mean changing a lot of other goals.

Here are some things to consider as you think about benchmarks:

- **Money.** Of course money is important, but remember that it comes at a cost. In general, earning more means risking more, working more, studying more, competing more, and showing more dedication to your job. Do you want to aim for wealth? Or stability? Or a specific income bracket?
- **Working conditions.** Is it important to you whether you work indoors or outdoors? Does physical risk bother you? How much does it matter whether you work in an office?
- **Family.** How would you like to balance family and job? Do you want to have children? Does it matter how much time you spend with your spouse and children? Do you want to live near your parents, siblings, or in-laws?
- **Geography.** Do you insist on living in a certain geographic region? Does it matter whether you live or work in a city, suburb, or rural area? Is it important that you live or work near a cultural center, a beach, mountains, good schools, or anything else? How much time are you willing to spend on your commute?
- **Employer.** Do you care whether you work for a large corporation, a smaller company, or yourself?
- **Education and training.** What is the level of education you want to reach? How much time and money are you willing to put into it? At what stage(s) in your career do you want to work on your education?
- **Definite job or career path.** Are you determined to take or aim for a certain job or follow a specific career path?

- **Shifts in career path.** Do you already know that you want to shift career paths at some point? For example, do you want to switch from practicing accounting to teaching accounting?

What Are Your Interests?

You'll be a lot more successful in your career if you do something that interests you. In fact, interest may be the most decisive factor in your success and satisfaction as a professional. Yet knowing which interests make for an ideal career can be tricky.

For example, being interested in baseball does not necessarily mean that you should—or can—become a professional baseball player. Yet, a seemingly frivolous interest may have potential. Your interest in baseball might help you pursue a career of coaching, journalism, health medicine, manufacturing of sports equipment, or broadcasting. Give all of your interests due consideration.

What if you are interested in computers? An interest does not mean you need to seek a job at Dell or IBM. Information technology reaches into almost every business in the country. You can turn your interest in computers into a career in health science in a hospital, in investment banking, television broadcasting, the military, advertising, sports administration . . . almost any field! Your interest can lead in directions you may never have considered. By looking at your values and benchmarks, you may discover a career that satisfies many interests.

Your Priorities

In this section, you've thought about your *values* and your *benchmarks*. Both are, by definition, important to you. As you thought about them, you probably thought of conflicts—values and benchmarks that can't happen at the same time. Just as Noreen probably can't run a horse farm and work on Wall Street, you will have to make some decisions.

Prioritizing—ranking values in order of importance—may remove certain values and benchmarks from your professional options. Or it may require you to organize your life so that you take care of the important things first, then move on to matters of lower priority.

prioritize put things in order of importance

Questions of Priority

As you determine your goals, you will also need to decide on the importance of each. Ask yourself the following questions as you prioritize your values, benchmarks, and goals:

- Which is more important in the long run?
- Which can wait? Which will be easier if done later?
- Which will make me a better person?
- How will this affect other people in my life?
- Do I really want to commit myself to this?
- What do I need to do before I get to this point?
- Will this prepare me for something else?

Professional Goals versus Personal Goals

One of life's big conflicts is the tug-of-war between professional goals and personal goals. The ideal would be to combine the two, but in reality, your profession is likely

> **"** *Know what you want to do, hold the thought firmly, and do every day what should be done, and every sunset will see you that much nearer to your goal.* **"**
>
> *Elbert Hubbard*
> *Nineteenth-Century Teacher, Editor, Printer, and Lecturer*

to pull you one way while your personal life pulls you another. Later in this chapter, you'll look at both kinds of goals and explore ways to bring them into a satisfying balance.

Look at the difficulties Noreen and Aaron will have maintaining their values as they pursue both personal and professional goals.

	Personal Goals	Professional Goals
Noreen	Own a nice house in the country	Work in a major investment bank
	Have a loving husband	Become department manager in 2 years
	Stay under 135 pounds	Commute less than 15 minutes
	Knit an afghan	Manage a mutual fund
	Own thoroughbred horses	Know all major financial software
	Earn an MBA	First-name basis with bank president
	Become vice president of a bank before 30	
Aaron	Own a house in the country	Teach high school art
	Have a loving wife and 3 children	Earn a Ph.D. in art history
	Attend a concert each month	Retire by age 60
	Read a book a week	Work with students after school every day
	Own a small airplane	Teach college course at night
	Spend a week overseas every year	Work at museum during summer
	Put kids through college	Earn Teacher of the Year award

Aaron and Noreen both have lofty personal and professional goals, but are they all realistic? By pursuing one, will they lose another? Can Noreen live on a horse farm and work on Wall Street? Can Aaron raise three children, teach at night, and study for a Ph.D.? Can Noreen become vice president? Is Aaron the type to study the stock market? Aaron and Noreen each has some thinking to do. Some personal and professional goals aren't compatible. Both people will need to do some prioritizing and scheduling to put their goals in order.

Ready . . . Aim . . . Goal!

As you can see in Figure 1.1, planning a goal takes several steps. Once you've given careful thought to your values, benchmarks, and priorities, you're almost ready to start setting personal and professional goals. Before you start, let's take a look at your strengths, abilities, and aptitudes. These are covered in the next section.

Figure 1.1 *The Steps to Creating a Goal*

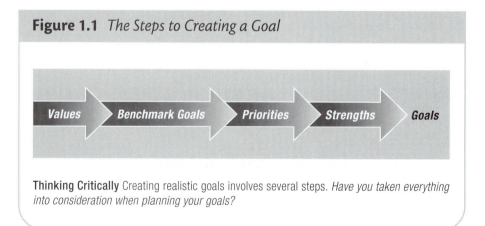

Thinking Critically Creating realistic goals involves several steps. *Have you taken everything into consideration when planning your goals?*

QUICK RECAP 1.1

ASSESSING WHAT YOU WANT

- Your value system helps determine your goals.
- Before you set goals, you should establish benchmark goals, that is, your most important goals.
- Benchmark goals are often set according to your firm preferences in salary, working conditions, family, workplace, preferred career, and efforts in education.
- Interests are important to consider in setting goals, but you need to think about where they might lead.
- You will need to prioritize your values, benchmarks, and goals in order to put goals in a logical order.

CHECK YOURSELF

1. Why is it important to understand your value system before setting your goals?
2. How are benchmark goals different from other goals?

Check your answers online at **www.mhhe.com/pace**.

Pace
ONLINE

BUSINESS VOCABULARY

benchmarks　points or standards from which you can measure or locate other things; in terms of goals, the important goals that are unlikely to change

goals　the ultimate aim of your efforts

prioritize　put things in order of importance

value system　the total of all your values and the way they work together

values　the basic beliefs that are important to you, the ones that guide your choices and tell you what is right or wrong

Assessing Your Strengths

What activities do you do well? What have you learned to do in school and in "real life"? What abilities just come to you naturally? What would you like to learn to do? The answers to these questions may not be as easy as you think. You probably have more strengths than you realize. Understanding your strengths will help you.

Feel your strength.   You've probably noticed that you are most likely to succeed when you're doing something you enjoy. If you let your interests and strengths guide your profession, you're all the more likely not only to succeed but also to enjoy your success. Assessing your strengths is definitely worthwhile.

Reading and Study Tip

Definitions
Look in this section for words that have similar meanings but are defined differently. Write the words and the difference in definition on a separate sheet of paper.

aptitude a natural ability to either do certain things or learn to do them, such as an aptitude for math or for working with others

skills a specific thing you have learned how to do

skills inventory a categorized list of things you can do, could do, and would like to do

Exploring Your Strengths

In the world of business, your strengths are the things you do well. Strengths can be separated into two general areas:

1. **Aptitudes.** Your natural abilities to do—or learn to do— certain things. Aptitudes cover general areas, such as working with children or working on mechanical operations.
2. **Skills.** Specific things you have learned how to do, such as explaining ideas to children or fixing office copiers.

You'll find it relatively easy to develop aptitudes into skills. By recognizing your aptitudes, you'll have a better idea which skills to pursue through education or training. When you have to learn a skill for which you have little aptitude, try to recognize that you may have to put in extra effort to learn it well.

Showing Off?

We are taught not to brag and to be humble about our gifts and talents. You should, however, know what these gifts and talents are. Otherwise, you might not feel—or act—confident. If you don't let others know what you can do, you may not be given the opportunity to use your skills. You should let your strengths be known in interviews, in performance reviews, and on résumés. In these cases, do not be humble!

Your Skills Inventory

Believe it or not, you may learn so much during your career that you'll lose track of your skills! When it comes time to write a résumé or go to a job interview, try to remember all the things you know how to do. To do this, start a **skills inventory**—a categorized list of things you can do, could do, and would like to do. You'll work on this inventory for the rest of your professional life. Keep adding to it as you remember skills you have, learn new skills, and think of skills you'd like to acquire. See Aaron's skills inventory, Figure 1.2, for an example.

Figure 1.2 *Aaron's Skills Inventory*

	Strengths	*Buildable Skills*	*Skill Resources*
Aptitudes	• Understanding people's problems • Art • Gardening • Working with youth	• Youth counseling, hotline counseling • Web site design • Organic gardening • Working with troubled teens	• State college, hotline training course • Adult education, college courses • Books • College courses, books
Interests	• Music • Art • Teaching	• Appreciation of soul music • African art • Corporate training	• Books, college course • Books, adult education
Current Skills	• Drawing and sculpting • Piano • Gardening • Teacher's aide	• Painting with acrylics • Guitar • Organic gardening • Secondary school certification	• Books, adult education, museum • Private tutor • Books • State college
Future Skills	• Read and perform music • Certification in secondary education • Speak Swahili	• Teaching choir • Guidance counseling	• College courses, private tutor, experience! • State college • Friends, instructional tapes, trip to Africa
Transferable Skills	• Writing • Learning from books • Can harmonize	• Journalism, creative writing • Lead a singing group	• Adult education, books • Church or community choir

Thinking Critically Study Aaron's aptitudes, interests, and current skills. *Are his future skills realistic? What other resources could he use to gain these skills?*

Start with five lists of skills:

- **Aptitudes.** List the aptitudes you have now and add to the list as you learn new skills.
- **Interests.** Your interests may include potential skills that you can quickly develop.
- **Current skills.** Keep adding to this list as you gain skills or remember the ones you already have. Note the skills that you will need to update or improve.
- Future skills. Unless you're in a dead-end job, you'll always find new skills that you need to learn. And if you are in a dead-end job, then mastering new skills can help you find a better one.
- **Transferable skills.** These are the basic skills that you carry from one kind of job to another, such as writing skills, interpersonal skills, knowledge of foreign languages, and so forth.

transferable skills skills that you can carry from one job to another, even from one profession to another, such as writing, languages, and so forth.

Now expand your inventory. For each of the aptitudes, interests, and skills you've listed, start two more categories:

- **Skills you can build on.** One skill is often the foundation for another skill. You can build an aptitude for mathematics into skills in calculus or statistics. An interest in nature might lead to skills in botany, ecology, or animal health care. A working knowledge of one software application can be built into skills with similar software.
- **Skill resources.** This is a list of places where you might go to learn new skills. Resources include schools, adult education programs, internships,

skill resources a list of places where you might go to learn new skills

books, videos, Web sites, professional associations, certification programs, mentors, friends, jobs, seminars, and company training programs.

Transferable Skills

Transferable skills, as mentioned above, are skills that you can carry from one job to another, even from one profession to another. They include such skills as writing, learning by reading, working with computers, speaking foreign languages, explaining things clearly to others, drawing and illustrating, and working with mathematics—to name just a few.

Transferable skills are good skills to have. They give you flexibility in your career and open the door to new opportunities. If you are dissatisfied with the path of your career, transferable skills give you a bridge to a new path. When a company's management needs to promote someone, they will first consider the person with transferable skills.

Benchmark Skills

benchmark skills the big skills that you definitely need for your career

In your skills inventory, start a page for **benchmark skills.** These are the skills that you definitely need for your career. You may have some already. You will certainly need more. Your list of benchmark skills may be short, but each skill demands a lot of expansion. You'll want to spend time exploring the resources for those skills.

> **Most people are so busy knocking themselves out trying to do everything they think they should do, they never get around to what they want to do.**
>
> *Kathleen Winsor*
> *Contemporary American Novelist*

The Helpful Strengths

Potential employers look for specific skills that fit specific jobs, but they also look for general strengths that enable you to put your skills to good use. Among these strengths are

- **Dedication.** Your willingness to put aside personal interests when your company needs extra effort from you.
- **Interpersonal skills.** The ability to work with other people, understand what they need, explain what you need, and be discrete and diplomatic in your interactions with them.
- **Leadership and management skills.** The ability to work with others, to make decisions that affect a team, and to know when to lead and when to follow.
- **Organizational skills.** The ability to plan ahead, work efficiently, prevent problems, avoid mistakes, and reach goals.
- **Intelligence.** The ability to figure things out, solve problems, and recognize the significance of situations.
- **A good attitude.** The internal drive to take up a challenge and dedicate enough energy to make your efforts pay off.

Look for Your Strengths

You may not think of all your aptitudes and skills. Some of your skills may come so easily that you don't even consider them skills. A good way to discover aptitudes and skills that you already have is to consult with someone else. Your friends and family may have suggestions. A school guidance or career counselor will know how to help you recognize hidden skills. Some employment agencies are prepared to help you identify your skills and express them to potential employers.

Future Strengths

During your career, you will grow. Every project and every job will teach you something. The companies you work for may train you. You may work on certification in certain areas. You may take courses at a college or university. You may attend seminars and conferences. No matter how much you know, you will always have more to learn. Use the following questions as a guide when planning what to learn next:

1. **What can you learn easily?** Look at your aptitudes. Look for skills that you can turn into more sophisticated skills. It's relatively easy to turn aptitudes and current skills into new skills.

2. **What would you *like* to learn?** Turning your interests into skills is easy because you find the subject interesting. Look at the "Interests" category in your skills and aptitudes inventory. Expand your inventory by exploring skills that can be developed from your interests.

3. **What training is available?** Whether you have a job, are looking for a job, or are still just thinking about a new job, you can probably find some kind of skill training somewhere in your community. Colleges offer continuing education courses. Some towns offer adult education. Professional and trade associations have local chapters that organize seminars. By joining one of these associations, you may be able to start a certification program. If you already have a job, talk to your human resources department or to a manager to find out what training is available. The company may help pay for the courses you take.

4. **What can you learn by reading?** A librarian can help you find books on specific careers, not only at your local library but also at other branches and online.

5. **What can you learn by doing?** By starting a project that requires more than just your current skills, you may be able pick up new skills. If you work on it with someone who already has the required skills, you may learn even more easily. Remember to add these skills to your inventory!

What to Do with Your Skills Inventory

Keep your skills inventory handy! You'll be using it a lot. Keep working on it. Continue thinking about your current skills and interests. Keep looking for sources of new skills. As your career path changes, update your inventory to reflect the skills you need.

Apply your inventory to your résumé. Your **résumé**—a summary, sometimes called a *curriculum vitae* or *cv,* of your education, training, skills, and professional experience—should list all relevant skills you can provide for an employer. Your inventory will help you remember all you have to offer.

Review your inventory before an interview. Remembering your skills after a job interview doesn't do you much good. (If that happens, find a way to mention those skills in your follow-up letter.) Prepare by reviewing your skills inventory before an interview. As you review your inventory, think about which skills might possibly be of interest to the employer. During the interview, be sure to ask if the company offers training. Interviewers like to hear these kinds of questions.

résumé a summary of your education, training, skills, and professional experience

❝ *Take care to get what you like or you will be forced to like what you get.* ❞

George Bernhard Shaw
Irish Nobel Prize–Winning Playwright and Social Commentator

Your Strengths and Your Career

Knowing your strengths will help you plan your career. At the same time, the course of your career will help you build new strengths. Strengths and careers drive each other forward. Look at your career as a process of improving your skills, and look at your skills as the building blocks of your career. In this way, your career will progress faster and be more satisfying.

QUICK RECAP 1.2

ASSESSING YOUR STRENGTHS

- Your strengths include not only your skills but also your aptitudes and your ability to learn new skills.
- A skills inventory will help you think about both the skills you have and the skills you would like to have.
- Benchmark skills are the important skills that you need for your profession.
- Transferable skills can help you succeed in different kinds of jobs.
- One skill is often the foundation of another skill.
- Look for skill resources—places you can learn new skills.
- Use your skills inventory both to build a good résumé and to prepare for job interviews.

CHECK YOURSELF

1. What is the difference between aptitudes and skills?
2. What is a skills inventory?

Check your answers online at www.mhhe.com/pace.

BUSINESS VOCABULARY

aptitude   a natural ability, or an ability to learn certain skills easily

benchmark skills   the big skills that you definitely need for your career

résumé   a summary of your education, training, skills, and professional experience

skill resources   a list of places where you might go to learn new skills

skills   a specific thing you have learned how to do

skills inventory   a categorized list of things you can do, could do, and would like to do

transferable skills   skills that you can carry from one job to another, even from one profession to another, such as writing, languages, etc and so forth

Setting Personal Goals

In the previous two sections, you've given some thought to what sort of career you want and have listed the strengths you need to pursue it. The next step is to set goals and lay out a plan for reaching them. You'll need to set personal goals (the goals that make you a better person) and professional goals (the goals that advance your career). By setting goals, you'll be able to advance step-by-step toward success rather than wandering around in confusion or giving up because your ultimate objective seems so far away.

Your goal: a better you.   For professional success, you need personal success, and that calls for personal goals. You will need to get your home life in order, get your body tuned up, learn new skills, meet new people, and prepare yourself for the rigors of the business world.

Personal Goals

In the first section of this chapter, we looked at the importance of using your values to determine your goals. But determining and achieving are two different things. Once your value system has told you which way to go, you need to set out a series of goals and a devise a methodical plan for achieving them.

A goal isn't really a goal unless you believe you can reach it. Obviously, the more distant the goal, the less certain you are of how to get there. You need distant goals, but you also need a series of goals between here and there. To reach your professional goals, you will have to reach some personal goals—goals that, once reached, make you a better person and a more powerful professional.

Reading and Study Tip

Parentheses
Parentheses add information or ideas to a sentence without interrupting its flow. Look at how parentheses are used in this section. Find two sentences where you could add an idea or put part of the sentence in parentheses.

Personal Goals to Professional Goals

If you have an idea of your professional goals, then you can start to think of the personal goals you need to reach first. If you aim to own a chain of computer software stores, your personal goals will probably include an education in information technology and business administration. Your first step, therefore, is to think about your professional goals (which we'll look at again in the next section) and then think about the goals that you, personally, have to reach in order to prepare yourself.

Types of Personal Goals

Various types of personal goals will help prepare you for professional goals.

- **Home goals.** What do you need to do to get your home life organized enough so that you don't worry about it at work?
- **Skill goals.** What skills, certifications, and levels of education will your professional goals require?
- **Health goals.** What do you need to do to ensure your health and fitness?

New Attitudes / New Opportunities

Meet Nyree Farmer. Nyree is a single mother of three young children. She is attending Indiana Business College for a degree in accounting and business administration, and works part time at night after school. Here is what Nyree has to say about . . .

Why she chose to go back to school. "I had already gone to college after high school, but not having my priorities straight, I dropped out. For me it was never a question of going, it was just basically when and what to do. I wanted to go back, it was just—when was a good time? After the first kid, it was hard, and after the second kid, it was harder, and it just kept getting harder. I had to tell myself after a certain point, 'It's not going to get any easier, so it's now or never.' "

Her goals for school and her career. "The main reason I went back was to get a degree. It's hard, but in the long run (in about five or six years from now), it will be worth it. I would like to be in a position where I am basically working for myself. Right now, my goal is to become an accountant with a firm and work on payroll or books. That's what I can see right now and I am trying not to look too far in advance. If I look too far in advance, I feel that when something comes my way, I may think it's under me. I don't want to start thinking that things are beneath me. I want to get my foot in the door somewhere, and I can always move up from there."

On the importance of having a support network. "I consider myself lucky because I have my family to back me up. There are a lot of single mothers that don't have their parents to baby-sit or they can't afford a babysitter. I'm sure it can be worked out in some way, but I know from standing in their shoes that it does get hard. I just want to let them know that *it can be done.* I try to be with my family when I'm out of school or not working. My schedule is hard on them, but I figured this was the best time to go back. I hope that it will make them think of their schooling. They will appreciate it a lot more when they are teenagers. When they start wanting stuff that will cost money, I'll be able to do that for them. They are my first priority: if they are home sick from school, that's a time that I can't go to school. But when they are in school, I have no other reason for *me* not to go to school, too."

- **Relationship goals.** What kinds of people should you try to meet? Who should you distance yourself from?
- **Emotional goals.** What do you need to do to keep yourself unstressed, focused on work, and undistracted by problems not related to work?
- **Financial goals.** How can you get your finances organized and headed in the right direction?

Think Small

A golfer's goal is to reach the end of an 18-hole green in as few strokes as possible. The more immediate goal, however, is to reach the *next* hole in as few strokes as possible. But that goal depends entirely on a sequence of smaller goals: focusing on a ball on a tee and swinging a club in a precise arc. If your personal goals seem unreachable, they are either totally unattainable or perfectly attainable but too far away to reach right now. Just as the golfer doesn't tee off with a swing for the 18th hole, you can't set your aim directly for a distant goal.

Start with a Reasonable Challenge

Set goals that are challenging but reachable. The challenge should include accomplishments that you are reasonably confident you can attain. If your goal is to establish a comprehensive insurance plan, then the accomplishments would include listing the things that need to be insured, estimating their value, and contacting an insurance agent.

Lists and Timelines

You may be surprised at how satisfying it is to check things off your list or timeline after you've completed them. Some people make a list of the next day's goals right before they go to bed. They find that this helps them sleep better. See Figure 1.3 for a sample list and timeline.

Set a Deadline

Timelines tend to end with deadlines. Or, rather, they begin with deadlines. Once you have a deadline, you can assemble your timeline in increments. Some people like the pressure of a deadline. It encourages them to work harder and faster. Deadlines also help you prioritize.

Figure 1.3 *Lists and Timelines*

Lists

Goal: Prepare for vacation
- Start packing clothes
- Stop mail
- Drop off gerbil at the pet sitter's
- Get car tuned and filled
- Finish packing
- Pack car
- Have a great time!

Goal: Start to get in shape

Sunday
   noon -throw away all cigarettes and ashtrays
Monday
   morn. -sign up at gym, work out 20 minutes
   noon -buy diet cookbook, find yoga class
Tuesday
   morn. -work out 20 minutes
   noon -celebrate 48 hours, no cigs
      -walk 15 minutes
   night -make low-fat meal from new cookbook
      -yoga class
Wednesday
   morn. -work out 20 minutes
      -make Dr. appointment for check-up
   noon -walk 20 minutes
   night -low-fat meal
Thursday
   morn. -work out 25 minutes
   noon -walk 25 minutes, buy tofu
   night -cook something with tofu, yoga class
Friday
   morn. -work out 30 minutes
   noon -walk 30 minutes
   night -one piece of pie to celebrate 5 days
      no cigs
Saturday
   morn. -work out 30 minutes, jog 20 minutes

Timelines   Calendar   Information   Addresses

Thinking Critically Lists and timelines break down the steps you need to take to reach your goals. *How do these lists make each task easier to accomplish?*

Be Serious

Your goals should be serious objectives. Use the following steps to help you accomplish your goals:

1. **Think about goals before you set them.** Are they attainable? Are they worth the effort? Do you really intend to reach them?
2. **Once you've set goals, stick to them.** Don't change your goals unless (a) they were wrong for you, (b) new circumstances require their change, or (c) you must absolutely admit defeat. In any of these cases, your next step is to set a new goal.
3. **Tell others.** Because (a) maybe they can help you; (b) out of embarrassment, you'll be less likely to abandon the goal; and (c) you'll want to show them that you could do it.
4. **Analyze failure.** If you abandon a goal, analyze what went wrong. Then set a more realistic goal.

Tips From a Mentor

Ten Tips on How to Network

• *Follow through* on leads you get. Make the call, write the e-mail, make an appointment, visit a location—do what it takes to make the next step.

• *Always carry your card* with you. You may want to quickly pass along your personal information at the gym, on a plane, or in a restaurant lobby. At the very least, keep pen and paper handy.

• *Don't wait too long.* Don't worry about appearing too eager. You don't want the house to be sold or the position to be filled before you "get around" to it.

• *Be persistent.* You may not make a connection the first time you try to network. Keep at it—it will pay off!

• *Go* places—go to staff parties, to seminars, to open houses, and to anywhere you might meet someone helpful.

• *Stay in contact* with former co-workers, neighbors, and classmates. You never know whom *they* may know.

• *Do your homework.* If you ask for help with something you could do by yourself, the person you asked will be less likely to offer help even when you do need it.

• *Thank* the person who connected you. If it resulted in a major change for you, such as getting a new job, consider sending a present, such as flowers or a gift certificate.

• *Always be polite and friendly.* Don't pester people. Some say that the squeaky wheel gets greased, but others say it gets replaced!

• *Talk even if you're not sure* the contact will get you what you want. The realtor selling a large house also may be renting out a small apartment.

Who Can Help?

Most people already have a support system in place. Family, friends, significant others, co-workers, and acquaintances are already involved in your life. Most of them want to help you. Yet, we all know people who do more to hinder than to help. Identify the helpful—and not-so-helpful—people in your support system.

People Who Help   You may already know some people who can give you the information, finances, guidance, products, and connections you need to reach your goals. You may need to find additional people to help. One of your goals, then, is to **network**—to put yourself in places where you might meet these people (a young professionals meeting, for example), and to tell people what you need in hopes that someone will recommend or introduce you to someone who can help.

network to put yourself in places where you might meet people who may help you

People Who Hinder   You don't need to network to find the people who stand between you and your goal. You already know them. They are the ones who tell you that you can't do it. They distract you from work. They call on the phone and knock on your door. They ask you to put aside your goal and help them with theirs.

What should you do with people who block your goals? It depends whether they are family, boss, co-worker, friend, or another kind of relation. Generally speaking, the best thing to do is explain your goal and ask them to help you.

Pace Points

You're Not Alone
Thank the people who support you by making them proud. For your family, friends, partners, and colleagues who have stood by you, your success is their success as well.

JUDGEMENT CALL

Support Network

Your Challenge
You have just started a new job with a company you respect. You are in a position where you can advance and eventually become a manager. Right now, however, you have to prove you can handle the responsibility by working late and spending some of your free time doing research, taking classes, and practicing your skills. Your partner is having a problem with your long hours and feels like you don't spend any time with him or her. You end up arguing when you are together. Your partner's attitude and behavior do not seem supportive of what you are trying to do. You really love this person, but he or she is making it very hard for you to achieve your goals.

The Possibilities
A. Give your partner an ultimatum, saying if he or she doesn't support you, then you will end the relationship.
B. Tell your partner that you are working hard now so you can have a better future together. Share your personal and professional goals with your partner and ask for support and remind him or her that it is only temporary.
C. Quit your job and stay at home to make your partner happy.
D. Ignore the situation and let your partner make his or her own decision to stay or go.

Your Solution
Choose the solution that you think will be most effective and write a few sentences explaining your opinion. Then check your answer with the answer on our Web site: **www.mhhe.com/pace.**

Looking Back

Every once in a while, stop and analyze your progress. Look at the goals you've already reached. Pat yourself on the back. Think about what you did right to reach that goal. Then, look at your progress toward goals you haven't reached yet. Ask yourself if you are where you should be at this time. Look for obstacles that could be removed. Try to foresee any future problems and brainstorm how to prevent or minimize them. Finally, think about goals you've failed to reach. Ask yourself what went wrong. Decide if you should try again and, if so, what you can do differently this time.

QUICK RECAP 1. 3

SETTING YOUR PERSONAL GOALS

- Personal goals help you reach professional goals.
- Personal goals include improvement in your home life, skills, health, relationships, emotions, and finances.
- Personal goals should be both obtainable and challenging.
- Lists, deadlines, and timelines will help you reach your goals.
- It's important to be sure you really want to achieve a goal before you commit yourself to it.
- It's helpful to seek out people who can help you, and to avoid those who hinder you.

CHECK YOURSELF

1. What is the connection between personal and professional goals?
2. What kinds of people can help you reach a goal?

Check your answers online at **www.mhhe.com/pace.**

BUSINESS VOCABULARY

network   to put yourself in places where you might meet people who may help you

Setting Your Professional Goals

You need to set professional goals. Without them, your career may bog down or seem to wander without direction. With them, you can lay out the steps you must take to move ahead. Your job also will demand goals, such as reaching a certain level of sales or learning new technologies. By always having a goal within reach, you'll know what you should be doing and where you should be going.

Goal + Goal = Success + Satisfaction.   You will always have goals in your short-term and long-term future. In this section, you'll look at some of the ways you can use goals to achieve professional success and satisfaction.

Professional Goals

Setting professional goals is a lot like setting the personal goals discussed in the previous section. Review the goal-setting steps below.

- Set goals that are challenging but achievable.
- Use lists and timetables of goals.
- Be serious about goals, committing yourself to them and analyzing the reasons for any failures.
- Find people who can help you, and avoid people who hold you back.

Professional goals relate directly to your job, your performance, your company, and the realities of business. You'll want to establish two types of goals. One kind is for your career, moving from where you are toward where you want to be. The other type involves getting your current job done.

Reading and Study Tip

Finding Key Terms
Words in *italics* and **boldface** draw attention to the words or phrases. Look for words and phrases in this section in italics and boldface. Why are these words especially important?

Career Goals

Your **career goals** should move you forward in your professional development. Don't forget the values mentioned in the first section of this chapter. Your goals should move you toward a higher salary or more free time or a more interesting job. . . . or whatever it is that fits your values.

To reach each career goal, you will usually go through four stages:

1. **Preparation.** How should you prepare yourself for your goals? What skills do you need? What evidence of competence, such as courses, degrees, and certification, do you need? What trade publications should you be reading? To whom should you be talking to learn more?
2. **Performance.** What performance goals can you set? Sales levels? Stage of product development? Machines maintained? Clients visited? A good performance review? Your company will probably have some way to measure your performance.
3. **Proof.** Who should know what you've accomplished? How will you prove it? (Memos? Activity reports? Diplomas?)

career goals goals that should move you forward in your professional development

Goals are simply tools to focus your energy in positive directions; these can be changed as your priorities change, new ones added, and others dropped.

O. Carl Simonton
Doctor, Author, and Lecturer

4. **Progress.** What is the progress you plan to make? A raise? A new title? A new job? An award? Your preparation, performance, and proof aim at this goal.

As soon as you've reached one goal, give yourself a pat on the back, take a quick look back at what you've accomplished, then set your sights on the next goal.

Job Goals

Your job will almost certainly involve goals. These **job goals** assure you and management that you are doing your job well. At an entry-level clerical position, the goal might be simply to keep accurate records and earn a good performance review at the end of the year. In a sales position, the goal might be to reach a certain level of sales. As a warehouse manager, you might be given the goal of computerizing the inventory system.

Some goals will be given to you. Some you will set yourself. They are equally important. A goal given to you becomes your goal. A goal you yourself set should be just as serious as the one your boss gave you.

Plan Your Attack

Companies don't normally set goals that are easy to reach, especially if you work in sales or management. If you can reach your own goals without much effort, you probably aren't being ambitious enough. Your goals should be challenging enough that you have to plan how to reach them. Follow this "plan of attack":

- List the steps you have to take to reach the goal.
- Set up a timetable for taking those steps.
- Think about the resources you need, the people who can help you, the places you'll need to go, the things you'll need to prepare.
- If other people are involved in the timetable, make sure they know how and when they fit in.
- As you proceed, maintain communication with others who need to monitor progress.
- If it becomes apparent that you won't reach the goal in time, inform the appropriate people.
- Foresee problems. Look for things that can go wrong, then take action to prevent them.

Be Realistic

You've probably heard the common advice to "reach for the stars." If you've ever tried it, you failed. Why? Because, obviously, the stars are just too far to reach.

If your goal is to leap from executive assistant to chief executive officer by the end of the year, you're just not going to make it. By all means, *aim* for the title of CEO, but set goals that you can effectively plan to reach. Look at the example of Tiffany Hicks. She has big career dreams but serious, reachable goals.

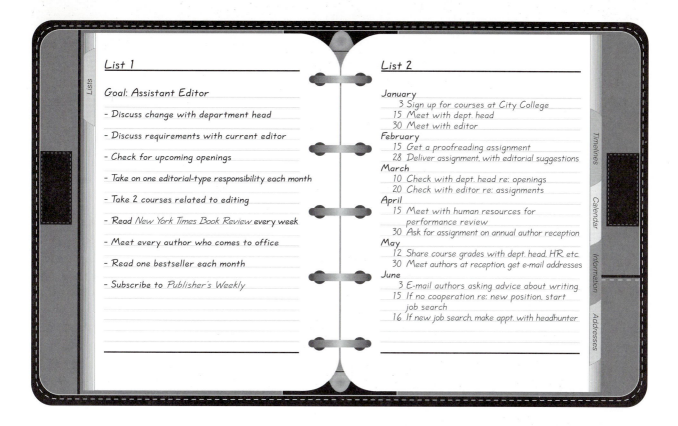

List 1

Goal: Assistant Editor

- Discuss change with department head
- Discuss requirements with current editor
- Check for upcoming openings
- Take on one editorial-type responsibility each month
- Take 2 courses related to editing
- Read *New York Times Book Review* every week
- Meet every author who comes to office
- Read one bestseller each month
- Subscribe to *Publisher's Weekly*

List 2

January
3 Sign up for courses at City College
15 Meet with dept. head
30 Meet with editor

February
15 Get a proofreading assignment
28 Deliver assignment, with editorial suggestions

March
10 Check with dept. head re: openings
20 Check with editor re: assignments

April
15 Meet with human resources for performance review
30 Ask for assignment on annual author reception

May
12 Share course grades with dept. head, HR etc.
30 Meet authors at reception, get e-mail addresses

June
3 E-mail authors asking advice about writing
15 If no cooperation re: new position, start job search
16 If new job search, make appt. with headhunter

JUDGEMENT CALL

Pigeon Holed

Your Challenge

You have been working in an entry-level position for almost a year. You have clearly proven your ability in your job and gotten great feedback from your boss and co-workers about your performance. You feel that you have paid your dues, gained experience, and learned how your company works. You feel you are ready to move up, have more responsibility, and make more money. The problem is, nothing seems to be happening. Everyone seems to be happy to keep you right where you are. What do you do?

The Possibilities

A. Quit your job without giving notice.

B. Keep doing your job well, keep quiet, and wait for a promotion.

C. March into your boss's office and threaten to file discrimination charges against him or her if you aren't given a better job, higher pay, and more responsibility.

D. Ask to meet with your boss and tell him or her how you feel. Suggest some of the responsibilities you would like and the position you want. Find out what the situation is and show that you are determined to move ahead.

Your Solution

Choose the possible solution that you think will be most effective and write a few sentences explaining your opinion. Then check your answer with the answer on our Web site: **www.mhhe.com/pace**.

Pace ONLINE

Your Company Structure

Before you set any career goals, look at the structure of your company. If you want to stay within the company, what upward pathways does it offer?

- Does the company offer a direct climb up to your ultimate goal? For example, in banking, you might follow this "career ladder" to the top: teller—head teller—assistant branch manager—branch manager—director of branch offices—vice president, bank operations—president.

- Does the company offer **lateral shifts** that move you over to a new kind of job rather than up the corporate ladder? For example, you might move from computer operation in the accounting department to a similar job at your company's manufacturing plant. The shift can position you for future advancement.

- Does your company offer a program for methodical advancement? Some companies may encourage you to keep moving up. Some may want you to "move around" among various facilities, departments, or even **subsidiaries** (other companies that your company owns).

Aim for the Stars

Reach for the stars and you will reach nothing. Aim for the stars and there's no telling how far you'll reach. In other words, dream big but keep your goals within reach. Challenge yourself. It's the best way to stay interested, get stronger, and achieve the success you seek.

QUICK RECAP 1.4

SETTING YOUR PROFESSIONAL GOALS

- Goals should be challenging but achievable.
- Lists and timetables will help you set and reach goals.
- Career goals move your career forward; job goals help you do your current job well.
- To reach career goals, you will normally need to prepare yourself, perform well, prove your performance, and make some kind of progress in your career.
- Whether you set a job goal or one is given to you, you must commit yourself to it.
- Planning is an important part of reaching a goal.
- Goals should be realistic but challenging.
- Career goals can be moves up through the company ranks or across, to different departments or workplaces.

CHECK YOURSELF

1. What is the difference between a career goal and a job goal?
2. What are some things to consider when planning to reach a goal?

Check your answers online at **www.mhhe.com/pace**.

BUSINESS VOCABULARY

career goals   goals that should move you forward in your professional development
job goals   goals that assure you and management that you are doing your job well
lateral shifts   shifts that move you over to a new kind of job rather than up the corporate ladder
subsidiaries   other companies that your company owns

Setting Your Attitude

Have you got an attitude? You probably do. It's almost impossible not to. But the real question should be whether you can *control* your attitude . . . or whether your attitude controls you. If you can control your attitude, your attitude becomes a powerful tool that can change drudgery to fun, despair to hope, and crisis to opportunity. It can make a bad job feel good, change failure to success, and pick up sadness from the pits and put it on a mountain peak in the sun.

Take control of your attitude. Make attitude work *for* you instead of *against* you. How? By understanding attitudes, their causes, and the ways to fix them when they go bad. This skill is as crucial to success as anything you learned in school.

You and Your Attitudes

What's an attitude? It's more than a mood. It's a way of seeing the world, a way of life. It's something inside you that determines how you see things outside you. It also determines what you do.

A *bad attitude* can lead you to do things wrong or badly or even to do nothing. It can leave you with no hope. It can rob you of your energy, your drive, your creativity, your humor, your personality, and your appreciation of your life. In short, it can defeat you. See Figure 1.4.

A *good attitude* can energize you, give you beautiful ideas, and leave you laughing in even the worst of circumstances. It can give you the courage to confront the biggest challenge—and not just confront it but rise above it and move beyond it. You can probably guess which kind of attitude is going to make you a success in your chosen profession.

Control Your Attitude . . . and Your Life

Attitudes happen. Sometimes they get pretty bad. That's life. But they aren't carved in stone. Attitudes are not permanent. They can be adjusted. To surrender to a bad attitude is to lose control of your life and yourself. Surrender to attitude doesn't have to happen.

Bad things happen to everyone at some point in each life. Even if you made mistakes or bad decisions in the past, being bitter will just make it worse. As long as you are alive, you have the chance to start anew. Keep up a positive attitude no matter what kind of attitude others give you. You have the power to make the best of a bad situation.

> *Nothing can stop the man with the right mental attitude from achieving his goal; nothing on earth can help the man with the wrong mental attitude.*
>
> **Thomas Jefferson**
> *Third President of the United States*

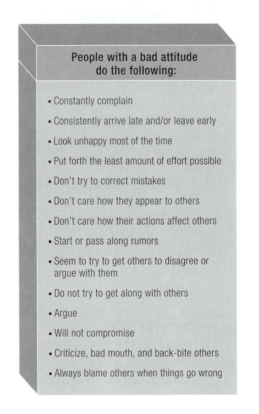

Figure 1.4 *Symptoms of a Bad Attitude*

People with a bad attitude do the following:

- Constantly complain
- Consistently arrive late and/or leave early
- Look unhappy most of the time
- Put forth the least amount of effort possible
- Don't try to correct mistakes
- Don't care how they appear to others
- Don't care how their actions affect others
- Start or pass along rumors
- Seem to try to get others to disagree or argue with them
- Do not try to get along with others
- Argue
- Will not compromise
- Criticize, bad mouth, and back-bite others
- Always blame others when things go wrong

Thinking Critically Most workplaces have at least one person with a bad attitude. Sometimes someone will seem to have a bad attitude simply because he displays a symptom from above. *Examine your own actions at work. Do you have any symptoms of a bad attitude?*

Assess Your Attitude

If your attitudes get the better of you in negative ways, the first step toward a better attitude is to assess your attitude. Simply placing blame will not help you move forward. Examine actions and thoughts that have brought you to where you are.

What Is the Source of Your Bad Attitude?

Put your feelings aside and ask yourself some serious questions.

- **Where did this attitude come from?** Was it fear of defeat? Was it rejection? Was it something you were thinking about? Was it stress from something else?
- **Has this attitude happened before?** If so, what caused it? What resulted from it? What cured it?
- **Was the cause really serious?** Or was it something that will go away? Something from your own mind? Something you will forget about someday? Is the cause bigger and stronger than you? Is your attitude based on an assumption?

What Is It Doing to You?

Watch others as they react to you. Try to step back and observe how your attitude is affecting your mood and your reactions to others.

- **How does this attitude affect your behavior?** Does it make you grumpy? Nasty? Sad? Short-tempered? Lacking energy? Withdrawn?
- **How is this attitude affecting others?** Is it driving away friends? Spoiling team spirit? Starting arguments? Preventing communication? Giving others bad attitudes?
- **Does it take up your time?** Is it causing you to think about things that have nothing to do with work? Does it make it hard for you to concentrate on your work? Does it stifle your creativity?

How Can You Change It?

Knowing you need to change and actually changing your attitude are two different things. Yet, knowing you should is the first step in doing it.

- **Can you put it in perspective?** How serious, really, is the cause of this attitude? What are some good reasons for a good attitude? Is the cause just a matter of pride, envy, self-pity, self-centeredness, or sense of failure?

> ❝ Anyone who has never made a mistake has never tried anything new. ❞
>
> *Albert Einstein*
> Nobel Prize–Winning Physicist and Mathematician

Tips From a Mentor

Ten Ways to Shake Off a Bad Attitude

- *Get enough sleep.* Take a nap or go to bed early if needed.

- *Talk about your stress* with friends, loved ones, or a counselor.

- *Exercise to release stress.* Even doing stretches can release those happiness-producing endorphins in your brain.

- *Try a new approach to work and life.* Do something differently than you have before.

- *Put things in perspective.* Look at your problems by thinking about the "Big Picture" of the important things in life: love, family and friends, health, and happiness.

- *Clear your head.* Pray or meditate, paint, sing, or enjoy hobbies to clear your mind and focus on positive things.

- *Simplify your life.* Focus on things you can control and don't worry about the rest.

- *Rise above the problem,* walk away from an aggravation, and put some distance between yourself and negativity.

- *Avoid negative people.* Simply complaining about a problem will only make you more unhappy. Negative people may be easy to talk to, but they won't help you.

- *Ask for help* from people with experience: your parents, mentors, employers, and role models. Ask how they keep from getting discouraged or negative.

- **Should you change something in your life?** Distance yourself from an unwanted friend? Change a bad habit? Work less and relax more? Work more and relax less? Change jobs?
- **Is there anything positive about the situation?** Could things have been worse? Might something negative have happened if a plan had succeeded? Does this put you in a good position for something else?

Failure

> *" Experience is not what happens to a man; it is what a man does with what happens to him. "*
>
> *Aldous Huxley*
> *British Author and Philosopher*

Often, a negative attitude comes because of some kind of failure—rejection, regret over a missed opportunity, mistakes made. Although appearances may seem otherwise, *everyone* has failed at one time or another. For example, newsman Peter Jennings was a high-school dropout; Thomas Edison failed over 1,000 times when trying to invent the light bulb; and Abraham Lincoln lost at least eight elections before being elected president. Each of these men is now known as successful. How did they overcome their failures? Much depended on their positive attitudes.

Feel, But Don't Flounder

When you fail, of course you will feel badly. Allow yourself a little time to experience all the emotions that accompany failure: anger, sadness, fear, self-pity, self-doubt, hopelessness, despair, bitterness, envy. If you deny your emotions, they will only show themselves in another way. The trick is to acknowledge both the failure and your emotions, then leave them behind.

Don't Let Failure Get You Down

Failure hurts. It's one of those things that nobody likes but everybody does. In fact, the people who fail the most are the people who strive for the most difficult goals. Failure to fail indicates failure to reach far enough.

So remember: The road to success is paved with failures and mistakes. Failure is an event, not a person. If you fail, it doesn't mean that *you* are a failure. It means you tried but didn't make it. With the right attitude, every failure makes you smarter and stronger and better equipped for success.

Make the Best of It

Again, failures and bad attitudes happen. But you don't have to surrender to them. You can actually put them to productive use! Attitude is what separates successful professionals from bitter, narrow-minded nine-to-fivers. Choose your attitude now and succeed!

- Use a bad attitude to reexamine your personal and professional goals.
- Think about how this incident has made you a stronger and better person.
- Let the attitude tell you how your life needs changing.

QUICK RECAP 1.5

SETTING YOUR ATTITUDE

- Attitude is a way of life.
- Bad attitude drains your energy, drive, creativity, personality, humor, and appreciation of life.
- Good attitude gives you energy, humor, and courage.
- Surrendering to a bad attitude is surrendering your life and yourself.
- You should assess bad attitudes by asking where they came from, what they do to you, and how you can change them.
- Use a failure to make yourself stronger and smarter.

CHECK YOURSELF

1. How can a good attitude help you succeed?
2. What are some techniques for improving attitude?

Check your answers online at **www.mhhe.com/pace.**

Chapter Summary

1.1 Assessing What You Want

Objective: Recognize what you want and set benchmarks for getting there.

In this section, you considered some of the values and goals that can help you better understand what you want in life and how to get there. You thought about benchmark goals and the many ways in which your interests and personal goals can relate to your career.

1.2 Assessing Your Strengths

Objectives: Assess your strengths, skills, and aptitudes and orient them to your goals.

In this section, you explored your aptitudes and skills to develop a skills inventory. You saw how you can tap skill resources to build current and future strengths into new skills. You studied the importance of benchmark skills and transferable skills. You also got a preview of the skills that employers want.

1.3 Setting Your Personal Goals

Objectives: Set personal goals and determine the steps you must take to reach them.

In this section, you saw how personal goals, such as new skills, good health, and organized finances, position you for professional success. You saw the value of using lists, deadlines, and timelines to plan your progress toward your goal. You learned the importance of taking your goals seriously and committing yourself to them. Finally, you read about how other people can help you or hinder you.

1.4 Setting Your Professional Goals

Objective: Set professional goals and determine the steps you must take to reach them.

In this section, you studied the importance of preparing to reach professional goals, then performing well on the job, proving your performance, and moving forward in your career. You learned some ways to "plan your attack" on your goals, and you learned that you can move laterally as well as up through your company.

1.5 Setting Your Attitude

Objective: Set your attitude on positive, take rejection and failure for what they're worth, and use your experiences to grow.

In this section, you considered how a bad attitude can defeat you and how a good attitude can energize and encourage you. You learned the importance of controlling your attitude and using failure to achieve success.

Business Vocabulary

- aptitudes (p. 10)
- benchmark goals (p. 5)
- benchmark skills (p. 12)
- benchmarks (p. 6)
- career goals (p. 21)
- goals (p. 5)
- job goals (p. 22)
- lateral shifts (p. 24)
- network (p. 19)
- prioritize (p. 7)
- résumé (p. 13)
- skill resources (p. 11)
- skills (p. 10)
- skills inventory (p. 10)
- subsidiaries (p. 24)
- transferable skills (p. 11)
- value system (p. 5)
- values (p. 4)

Key Concept Review

1. What is the difference between benchmark goals and benchmark skills? (1.1)

2. Why is it important to understand your value system before you set your goals? (1.1)

3. Why should you keep a skills inventory? (1.2)

4. What are skill resources and how can you use them? (1.2)

5. How are personal goals important to professional success? (1.3)

6. What should you do about people who hold you back from your goals? (1.3)

7. How can planning help you reach your job goals? (1.4)

8. How difficult should goals be? (1.4)

9. How can a bad attitude defeat you? (1.5)

10. Why should you not let failure discourage you? (1.5)

Online Project

Skills Resources

Think about the benchmark skills you need for your profession and career. Use a search engine to find online skills resources that can help you build those benchmark skills.

Step Up the Pace

CASE A   Planning to Reach a Goal

Your small company has been bought by a major international corporation. Your boss has found another job, her boss has retired, and you've been given the goal of integrating your company's computer system with the parent company's. You know little or nothing about computer systems. Reaching this goal will be a huge step in your career. Failing to reach it could cost you your job.

What To Do

1. Develop a list of people who can help you.
2. Plan the steps to take to coordinate and communicate with others in this project.

CASE B   Adjusting a Colleague's Attitude

Your sales team was doing a great job of preparing a presentation for an important customer. You thought you would be called on to be team leader, but weren't. You fall into a deep depression. You no longer care about the presentation. You think about quitting your job, but your team needs you for the computer graphics part of the presentation.

What to Do

1. Write five questions you'd ask yourself to try to understand your attitude.
2. List five things you could do to adjust your attitude.

Netiquette

With the ever-increasing use—and importance—of e-mail in business, you need to learn network etiquette, or "netiquette." Study the tips below.

- Keep your message brief and to the point.
- Write your topic in the subject line so your reader(s) can find your note again quickly.
- Avoid typing in all caps (all capital letters). This is the equivalent of yelling.
- Sparingly use abbreviations, for example, BTW (by the way) and FYI (for your information). Avoid emoticons (such as ☺) in business e-mail.
- Copy everyone involved including superiors, if appropriate. This keeps everyone informed and saves you time.
- Don't assume any messages are private. E-mail can be easily forwarded. Also, a company's systems administrators can monitor anyone's e-mail in the network.
- Be careful of your phrasing. You cannot convey tone by e-mail. A joking comment may be misread as an insult.
- When forwarding or replying to a message, delete any unnecessary or sensitive text.
- Consider using a brief signature listing your title and phone number or extension.
- Don't forward chain letters or jokes to business associates unless they have directly expressed an interest in the cause or information.

Proofread the e-mail below. Circle mistakes in it.

Mail

New Message

Send | Save Draft | Attach | Tools | Cancel

From: M_White@XYinc.com

To: S_Barr, L_Jones, D_Mackey, S_Mull, N_Yona

Cc:

Bcc:

Subject: New logo meeting

```
Hi guys,

Just wanted you to know that there will be a meeting in the boardroom
for everyone involved in the new logo project. VP Veep will lead the
meeting. Please be there in time to start by 10 A.M. That way we can
be sure to finish by lunchtime ☺. Bring pencil, paper, and ONLY PRE-
APPROVED sketches. BTW, if you have a time conflict, let me or Ms. Veep
know ASAP! Below is the agenda.

Mike

<<Dear Mike,
<<Here is the agenda for the logo meeting. Unless you have any
corrections or additions, please pass <<this along when we determine
where and when to meet. Thanks!
<<—Review logo guidelines
<<—Present all pre-approved sketches
<<—Suggest changes to current sketches (if needed)
<<—Vote
<<Veronica Veep, Vice-President of XY, Inc.
<<ext. 3351
```

Items you should have circled include the subject line, greeting, text in all caps, smiley face, and extra text in the attached e-mail by Ms. Veep. There may be more that you found as well.

Exercise: On another sheet of paper, rewrite the e-mail from the previous page so that it better follows the rules of netiquette. Feel free to create new information, such as the sender's position.

Manage Time, Stress, Money, and Yourself

What Will You Do?

2.1 Assessing Your Lifestyle Look for patterns of behavior that will help or hurt your efforts to succeed.

2.2 Managing Your Time Learn to deal with procrastination and manage your time through planning, scheduling, and multitasking.

2.3 Managing Your Stress Examine the sources of stress and the best ways to deal with them.

2.4 Managing Your Money Learn to manage your finances by avoiding debt, keeping up with taxes, using insurance to minimize risk, and working with an effective budget.

2.5 Managing Yourself Assess your habits and opportunities, then make strategic changes.

Why Do You Need to Know This?

Life is not simple these days. Everyone has to juggle a lot at home and at work. But juggling works only if you keep things moving and organized. If things get out of order, everything collapses. To keep yourself organized, you must organize your time, your money, and your life.

Chapter Objectives

After completing this chapter, you will be able to:

- Identify aspects of your lifestyle that work for or against your career.

- Use your time wisely and productively.

- Control your stress level by understanding what causes stress.

- Keep your finances in order and put your money to good use.

- Make strategic changes in your life in order to become more productive and more satisfied.

Set the *Pace*

Manage Time, Stress, Money, and Yourself Think about your life as it was several years ago, at an earlier stage in your personal development.

- What were some habits that you had then but don't have now?
- Who managed your time?
- What did you do in stressful situations?
- How have you changed since then?

Activity In the journal section of your career portfolio, write a few paragraphs about how your life has changed since that earlier stage. Write about the differences in your behavior, your schedule, your approach to stress, and your attitude toward money. Then write a couple of paragraphs about how you expect to change over the next few years.

Assessing Your Lifestyle

How long has it been since you stepped back and took a serious look at your lifestyle? This is something you need to do now and then. You've already changed a lot in your lifetime, and you will naturally change more as you mature. You're already at an age where you can be rational about your personal development. You can look at your life and see what needs changing.

Approaching Self-Improvement.   There's no better time than now to take a look at your habits and general behavior and see what could use a little improvement. Just as you periodically upgrade your car, stereo, and computer, you need to upgrade yourself. This section will help you figure out how.

Reading and Study Tip

Summary

The "Quick Recap" feature at the end of each section summarizes the main points of the section into a bulleted list. To *summarize* is to sum up key ideas or points without going into the details. Choose one paragraph in this section. On a separate sheet of paper, summarize the key points addressed in that paragraph.

patterns of behavior things you tend to do fairly regularly, things that might be called habits

❝ *No one can remember more than three points.* ❞

Philip Crosby
Writer and Consultant
on Quality Management

Patterns of Behavior

Have you ever analyzed your daily and weekly life for **patterns of behavior**—things you tend to do fairly regularly, things that might be called habits? A complete analysis of your patterns of behavior might produce enough information to fill a book. It might include things like:

- Plans day while driving to work.
- Stares out window for seven minutes each hour.
- Checks e-mail every 42 minutes.
- Always says *please* and *thank you.*
- Feels sleepy after lunch.

You don't have to fill a book to produce a useful analysis of your patterns of behavior. A few minutes of thought will do much to reveal behavior that is influencing your professional life.

Where to Look for Patterns of Behavior

Your way of life is built on your patterns of behavior. So, where do you start your analysis? Several kinds of behavior patterns are important to your personal and professional development:

- **Personal habits:** bathing, grooming, dressing, exercising, eating, drinking, relaxing, appreciating beauty, being thankful, praying, meditating.
- **Communication:** relating to friends and co-workers, answering mail, returning phone calls, reporting activities, listening to others, knowing what to put in writing, revising written work.
- **Organization:** keeping records, filing information, planning, scheduling, using lists, preparing alternative plans, arriving on time, paying bills on time.
- **Learning:** about new technologies, industry news, new techniques . . . and yourself.
- **Discipline:** working steadily, staying focused, finishing projects, resisting temptation, suffering short-term pain for long-term gain.
- **Financial:** Avoiding credit card debt, controlling spending, investing carefully, saving for the future, balancing your checkbook, using insurance.

Approaches to Improvement

As you analyze your patterns of behavior, look for three ways to improve them. In so doing, you will make yourself a more powerful professional.

- **Improve good patterns.** If you already plan your day, try planning two days. If you answer e-mail promptly, get in the habit of revising it before you send it. Is there more technology you could be learning?
- **Minimize unproductive patterns.** If you tend to procrastinate, do it less. If you tend to leave projects unfinished, try to finish at least the next one you work on.
- **Eliminate destructive patterns.** Stop smoking. Eat less. Go to bed earlier so you can wake up on time. Make sacrifices to pay off debts.

Take Care of Your Physical Condition

You've been hearing it all your life: Eat a balanced diet. Get plenty of exercise. Don't smoke. Say no to drugs. Get a check-up. Brush your teeth. Don't chew your nails. Sit up straight. . . . It's a long list, and you know it well. We won't review it here except to say that your physical condition really does make a difference. When you're healthy and in shape, you think better, work better, look better, and, of course, feel better. You'll do better personally and professionally.

Relationships

Relationships with other people—friends and family as well as co-workers—can make or break you. Most, of course, will do neither, but some will keep you from being all you can be. Others will help you be more than you are.

Who's Holding You Back?

Friends are great to have, and it's great to be friends with a variety of people. Unfortunately, some people can hold you back. One may bring out the worst of your habits. Another may waste your workday with endless conversation. Another may drag you into office gossip and politics. Another may give you bad advice and insist that you take it. Another may always be asking for favors.

It's very hard to deal with these kinds of relationships. There are no simple solutions. You have to do something about them. Avoiding these friends may not solve the problem. You may have to talk with them, explain the problem, and ask them to cooperate. Real friends will understand. In some cases, you may have to end the relationship.

Who Can Help You?

As your career takes you to new jobs, new offices, and new places, you'll find people who know your business or your profession better than you do. The supervisors and vice presidents that you report to should be more than glad to help you do your job better. That's their job. The peers you work with should help you be a more productive part of their team. Executive assistants and mail clerks often know the ins and outs of the office.

When any of these people show a willingness to help you, they are your friends and should be treated as such. Thank them, remember them, and return the favor when you can. When you meet new people in your workplace, do what you can to help them.

> *Habit is necessary; it is the habit of having habits, of turning a trail into a rut, that must be incessantly fought against if one is to remain alive.*
>
> **Edith Wharton**
> *Nineteenth-Century Author*

> *I don't believe in circumstances. The people who get on in this world are the people who get up and look for the circumstances they want, and if they can't find them, make them.*
>
> **George Bernard Shaw**
> *Irish Nobel Prize–Winning Playwright and Social Commentator*

Distraction

Your Challenge

You have a major assignment to do for work and have had no time to focus on it. All day you have been answering calls, solving problems for your boss, talking with clients, and managing paperwork people keep dropping on your desk. You managed to finish your research, but you still need to write a report. You are tired, hungry, and losing focus. You decided to bring your work home but find your kids bouncing off the walls and your partner in a cranky mood. You don't know what to do to avoid being distracted.

The Possibilities

A. You visit with your family, then ask your partner to take the kids to a movie so you can have your work done in time to spend time with him or her later. While they are out, you take time to eat, change, unplug the phone, and set yourself up in a quiet space to finish your report.

B. You lock yourself in your room and start on the report as soon as you get home—without saying hello, unwinding, or eating. Your kids keep banging on the door wanting you to solve an argument and your partner is complaining he or she can't deal with them. You do your best to ignore them and focus even though you are uncomfortable and light-headed. You crank out a report before falling asleep at your desk.

C. You get home and immediately start picking up after the kids, fixing dinner, and helping them with homework while your partner watches TV. You start the report at 10:00 p.m. and don't finish until after midnight. You figure you can get caught up on sleep on the weekend. You hope that you can stay awake through your staff meeting.

D. You get home and the TV's on so you get sucked into watching a show with the kids. Once the kids are in bed, a friend calls and you end up chatting with him or her until 10:00 p.m. You give up on waiting for a quiet moment to work and decide to get up early tomorrow morning to finish your work, not thinking about the distractions of getting the kids ready for school.

Your Solution

Choose the solution that you think will be most effective and write a few sentences explaining your opinion. Then check your answer with the answer on our Web site: www.mhhe.com/pace.

Find a Mentor

mentor a professional who is willing to guide you through your job and teach you about the business

With a little luck, you might find a **mentor** who is willing to guide you through your job and teach you about your business. A good mentor is a treasure to appreciate and keep. A mentor can teach what you didn't learn in school by giving you the wisdom he or she has gained through years of experience. When you find that someone really wants to help you and teach you, accept the help and recognize the respect you owe this person.

Don't Beat Yourself Up

When you assess your patterns of behavior, you may not like many of the things you see. Don't punish yourself or get discouraged. Use the information you learn about yourself to make your life better. Self-improvement is an ongoing process. You can't do it all at once—take one step at a time. See Figure 2.1 for a summary on where to start.

Figure 2.1 *Summary of Behavior Patterns*

By...	You can...
Analyzing your patterns of behavior	Identify what in your life you need to change.
Identifying good, unproductive, or destructive patterns	Know which behavior to maximize, minimize, or eliminate.
Keeping physically fit	Think, work, look, and feel better.
Assessing your relationships	See who's holding you back and who's helping you along.
Looking for people who can help you	Get help when you need it.
Accepting advice from a mentor	Learn your profession faster and better.

Thinking Critically The results you get from assessing your patterns of behavior are well worth the effort. *What one item on the chart can you do now to improve your life?*

QUICK RECAP 2.1

ASSESSING YOUR LIFESTYLE

- Your patterns of behavior influence your professional life.
- In assessing your patterns of behavior, look at the ways you take care of yourself, communicate, organize, learn, work with discipline, and take care of your finances.
- You can improve your professional performance by improving your good behavior patterns, minimizing your unproductive behavior patterns, and eliminating your destructive behavior patterns.
- It really is important to take care of your physical condition.
- Confront friends who make your personal or professional life more difficult, and appreciate friends who help you improve.

CHECK YOURSELF

1. What kinds of patterns of behavior influence your professional life?
2. What should you do about a co-worker who takes up your time with office gossip?

Check your answers online at **www.mhhe.com/pace.** *Pace* ONLINE

BUSINESS VOCABULARY

mentor   a professional who is willing to guide you through your job and teach you about the business
patterns of behavior   things you tend to do fairly regularly, things that might be called habits

Managing Your Time

Have you got time? Or, has time got you? If time is controlling your life, rather than you controlling your time, you're going to find it difficult to get much done. Sometimes it seems the world plots to distract you, get in your way, hold you back, and leave your head spinning. By the end of the day, you've gotten nothing done. Time got away from you and left nothing behind but a mess on your desk.

Time Management. If you make a determined effort, you can manage your time and use it to your advantage. All it takes is some planning, some organization, some efficiency, and a little discipline. This section should help you tame your time and make it a tool you can use to your professional benefit.

Reading and Study Tip

Repetition
Repetition can help stress the importance of an idea or thought. When used intentionally, it gets your attention and helps you learn the information being repeated. Find the repeated words in this section. Write down the ideas you think are being stressed.

> **An unhurried sense of time is in itself a form of wealth.**
>
> Bonnie Friedman
> *Contemporary Author*

The Control of Time

You can't really control time, of course. It keeps passing just as surely and regularly as the ticking of a clock. Nothing stops it. Nothing slows it down. Nothing guarantees that it leads you where you want to go. But you can *manage* time. You can use your time to be productive. To do so, you need to get going, keep going, stay on track, and step by step get things done.

Two Laws of Work and Time

Good managers recognize two laws of work and time:

1. The amount of work that must be done will tend to be done in the time available.
2. The amount of work that must be done will tend to fill all the time available.

In other words, if you must get the job done by 3:00, you will. But if you have three days to get the job done, it will take three days (with most of the work done in the last hours, not the first). Good time managers work with and against both of these tendencies.

1. They don't try to cram too much work into too little time, because that tends to add up to a job poorly done.
2. They don't allow too much time for the job, because then the job will take too long to do.

Efficiency and Effectiveness

efficiency the ratio of input to output;, that is, the amount of energy that is put into the production of something compared to the quantity actually produced

Efficiency is the production of something with little waste or unnecessary effort. Inefficiency means spending more energy producing something than it's worth. Time spent efficiently is time spent without waste or too much effort. An efficient worker focuses energy on an end result.

Effectiveness is the extent to which efforts produce expected results. Time spent effectively is time that produces what it was supposed to produce. An effective worker produces what he or she sets out to produce.

The Obstacles

How we spend our time is something everyone needs to try to improve. Many factors tend to cut down your efficiency and effectiveness. Among them are:

- Procrastination
- Lack of organization
- Distractions
- Lack of effort
- Doing too much or too many things at once
- Bad work habits

> *Time is the coin of your life. It is the only coin you have, and only you can determine how it will be spent. Be careful lest you let other people spend it for you.*
>
> *Carl Sandburg*
> *Poet, Lecturer, and Folk-singer*

Procrastination

Procrastination is the act of putting off until later what you should do now. Everybody has the urge to procrastinate, but some people—including good professionals—put that urge aside and do what they must do. If you have the habit of procrastinating, you must get control of it. See the feature "Tips from a Mentor" for strategies that might help.

Organize Your Time

In Chapter One you saw some of the benefits of using to-do lists and timetables. You'll find that these are especially helpful tools in time management. Here are some tips for better lists and timetables:

- Make it a habit to start all projects and days with a list of steps to take and things to do.
- Use the written list to sort activities into a logical order for your day.
- Make the list into a timetable by setting deadlines for each step or activity.
- Timetables must be reasonable. Don't plan too much. Build in time for breaks, meetings, and interruptions.
- If you tend to hit obstacles, let your list include expected obstacles and notes on how you will deal with them.
- Work on tomorrow's list today, so you don't forget things.
- Organize lists according to your goals.

Plan, Plan, Plan   Lack of planning may be the biggest detractor from efficiency. Planning gets projects started on time. It gets things done in the right order. It prevents projects from drifting off course because some part of it wasn't ready. It makes sure everybody knows what to do and when to do it. It helps prevent mistakes and misunderstandings. It makes you look good—like a good time manager and a good professional.

> *Time is an illusion. Lunchtime doubly so.*
>
> *Douglas Adams*
> *British Author and Humorist*

Start with a Plan   As you can see from the sample plan in Figure 2.2, planning can involve a simple list of activities, steps, or goals, or it can be a major project involving whole departments over the course of weeks. You yourself should plan every day and every project. Dedicate the first hour of each day to planning. Use the

Ten Tips to Beating Procrastination

- *Start immediately.* Do just one small thing to start the project.

- *Make a plan.* Rather than actually start the project, plan it. Make a list or timetable.

- *Get creative!* Consider **delegating** (assigning the project to someone else) or asking for help.

- *Watch for pitfalls.* List the things you tend to do when you procrastinate, such as make coffee, get into conversations, check e-mail, and so forth. Then do those things before you sit down to work.

- *Lessen interruptions.* List the things that you let interrupt you, such as phone calls and e-mail. Block those things if you can.

- *Do a part.* Do just a little of the project, telling yourself you'll procrastinate later.

- *Trick yourself!* Come up with a reward you receive only if you finish the project on time, like a movie, a game of golf, or a night out with friends.

- *Schedule your procrastination!* Work for an hour, then give yourself 15 minutes to check e-mail and have coffee. Work for another two hours, then give yourself 20 minutes to go for a walk. Only give yourself the procrastination time if you've stuck to your schedule.

- *Push yourself.* Once you stop working, it's hard to start again. Use your bursts of motivation wisely. If you feel the urge to stop working and do something else, make yourself work 10 minutes longer, 20 minutes, 30 minutes, or until you finish.

- *Stay focused.* If you find yourself daydreaming, doodling, or "zoning out" at your computer, take a mini break. Stretch your arms and legs, take a deep breath, grab a glass of water, and get right back to work.

---

delegating assigning a project, responsibility, or authority to someone else

whole hour, if needed. Think of all the details involved in your day. It might be a good idea to start your plan the night before with a to-do list. It may help keep you from worrying when you should be sleeping. Your plan should include

- A timetable.
- A list of all people involved.
- A list of all materials and documents involved.
- **Contingencies,** that is, alternate plans in case things go wrong.
- Foreseeable obstacles.
- Agendas for meetings and important phone calls.

contingency an alternate plan to be used if things go wrong

prioritize rate the importance of a task

Prioritize   Sort your plan or to-do list into priorities so that you do the most important things at the appropriate time. To **prioritize** means to rate the importance of a task. This may mean doing the most important things first, so you're sure they get done. It may mean doing them last, so you have all the necessary information, documents, materials, and so forth. It may mean doing them in a certain logical order.

Figure 2.2 *Plan for the AceTek Visit*

When		Do What	Who	With
Monday April 10	a.m.	• Confirm AceTek team's visit to our office on Mon. April 17 • Confirm times and ask what they would like added to their schedule	Dave	Call or e-mail (offer 19th or 24th as alternatives if needed)
	1:30 p.m.	• Meet with senior staff to plan agenda for AceTek and delegate preparations	Dave leads mtg., Mark, Marty, Rose, Adam	
Tuesday April 11		• Make reservations at Marcelita's for lunch on mtg. day (if not available, try Gamekeeper's Inn) • Inform cleaning staff of extra work	Kathy	
		• Plan agenda from mtg suggestions • Route agenda to sr. staff for approval • Retrieve agenda by end of day	Dave	Routing slip
Wednesday April 12	9:30	• Plan presentation and delegate as needed	Mark's team, Rose's team	
		• Finalize agenda • Send to sr. staff and AceTek team	Dave Kathy	
Thursday April 13		• Teams meet individually to fine-tune their parts in the presentation	Mark's team, Rose's team	
Friday April 14	10:00	• All teams meet to practice presentation	Dave, Mark's team Rose's team	Bring quotes, prototypes, etc.
		• Confirm reservations	Kathy	Confirm final count with Dave
Saturday April 15		• Meet if needed for final preparation	As needed	As needed
Monday April 17		• SEE AGENDA to be added		

Thinking Critically CreatTech Company is about to get a visit from a company that is thinking of hiring them. CreatTech wants to make sure they get the business, so they make a plan for how to prepare for the AceTek visit. *What information will be on the agenda for Monday, April 17?*

Dr. Joe Pace
SELF SCHEDULE

"Whenever possible, build your schedule around your personal needs. If you know you are more focused in the morning, schedule time for work that requires your concentration then. Know when you are most effective and use that time effectively."

If there are certain times during the day when you are especially productive, do important things then.

Delegate Good managers delegate certain activities to others. The more you can delegate, the more you yourself can do. Delegating frees your time, allowing you to get more done. Learn to trust others with appropriate assignments. Make sure, however, that all appropriate people know: (a) what you're doing and (b) what they should be doing. Make communication part of your plan when you delegate tasks.

Do It Right the First Time You've probably heard the saying, "If you don't have time to do it right the first time, you definitely don't have time to do it over again." In other words, working too fast will result in mistakes or shoddy work. In the long run, mistakes and poor quality waste time and reduce efficiency. As you work, pause to check for accuracy and quality.

❝ *Don't say you don't have enough time. You have exactly the same number of hours per day that were given to Helen Keller, Pasteur, Michelangelo, Mother Teresa, Leonardo da Vinci, Thomas Jefferson, and Albert Einstein.* ❞

H. Jackson Brown
Contemporary Author

Scheduling

Your Challenge

You have a lot of responsibilities at work so you decide to create a schedule for yourself. You want to budget the time so every task gets a fair share of your time. You want to make sure that the schedule works with everyone else's. You want your schedule to suit your needs and availability, but you also want the schedule to actually work.

The Possibilities

A. Write your ideal schedule, how you want everything to fit into your day, exactly how much time it should take, and give it to other people to follow.

B. Write a loose schedule with the times you think people are free and the amount of time you think things take and just use it as a guideline while you work hour-by-hour.

C. Talk to your boss, customers, and co-workers. Work out the details of their day and ask them how long things take for them. Work in driving times and extra time if you travel. Then work out your own needs and find a compromise between the two. Ask for help to resolve scheduling conflicts.

D. Make a schedule with your professional needs as a priority. Show it to your boss, co-workers, and customers, pointing out the time slots when you'll be available.

Your Solution

Choose the solution that you think will be most effective and write a few sentences explaining your opinion. Then check your answer with the answer on our Web site: **www.mhhe.com/pace**.

Dr. Joe Pace
FOCUS

"To help you stay focused on what you are doing, write down a one-line goal for the task you are about to do. If the phone rings, you get distracted, or your thoughts start to wander, refer to your note to help you stay on track. Don't start another task until you have met your goal and crossed out your note."

multitasking the activity of working on more than one task at a time

Distractions

Stopping and re-starting projects tends to waste time. Once you've started a task, try to stick to it until it's done. Avoid interruptions by not answering the phone and by asking others not to bother you until a certain time. Don't let unfinished projects pile up on your desk. If you just put one project aside, file it, then start on the next task. Don't try to do two or more projects at the same time.

Multitasking

Multitasking is the activity of working on more than one task at a time. It's impossible for your brain to do two things at once. If you're trying to talk on the phone while writing a report, your brain is actually going back and forth between the two tasks—and probably not doing either very well.

Multitasking raises your efficiency only when one of the tasks is inactive or automatic. For example, if you're on the phone and someone puts you on hold, use the time to tinker with your to-do list, quickly check your e-mail, or proofread something you've written. You can work while on a plane, phone people from airport gates, read during lunch, or expand a meeting agenda while waiting for others to arrive.

Bad Work Habits

Bad work habits include anything you do that stops you from working, causes errors in your work, or in any other way cuts down on your efficiency or effectiveness. Your time is much better spent if you can turn those bad habits into good habits. See

Figure 2.3 *Replace Bad Habits*

Bad Habit to Replace	Instead	By...
Procrastinating	Do it now	Starting with the easiest job
Daydreaming	Focus	Concentrating on just one task
Starting without a plan	Plan	Writing a to-do list each day
Failing to communicate with others who are involved	Communicate	Touching base with each person regularly
Wasting time on unproductive activities	Stick to the task and finish it	Avoiding or eliminating distractions
Letting others distract you	Avoid interruptions	Politely telling them you'll have a talk later (and get back to them when you finish)
Working too fast and thus making mistakes	Do it right the first time	Working carefully
Working haphazardly, that is, not doing things in a logical order	Work methodically	Setting a timetable and sticking to it
Trying to do everything yourself	Delegate	Asking others for help

Thinking Critically The best way to stop doing a bad habit is to replace it with a good habit. *What bad habit do you need to replace?*

Figure 2.3 for a list of typical bad habits—and examples of how to replace them with good habits.

Efficient, Effective Meetings

Meetings are a necessary part of business and a good way for several people to communicate and share ideas. But they also can waste a lot of time. If you have any control over the meetings you attend, you can contribute to their effectiveness and efficiency.

- **Stick to an agenda.** To prepare others, distribute the agenda well before the meeting. Use the agenda as a reason to get wayward discussions back on track.
- **Start on time,** even if some people have not arrived. If you wait, even fewer people will be on time for the next meeting.
- **Take control.** If you're running the meeting, don't be afraid to rap the table to stop a useless discussion and bring the meeting back to the agenda. Direct people to speak, and stop them from going on too long by thanking them. Even if you're not chairing the meeting, fill a power vacuum by asking people to stick to the agenda and asking specific people for input.
- **Don't hold a meeting,** if possible. Settle it by phone, e-mail, or a quick conversation in the hall.
- **End the meeting at a predetermined time,** unless it's still proving productive for all.

Personal Time

Sometimes it may seem that your company doesn't want you to have a personal life. To keep your life in balance, make sure that you are getting enough time in your day to have a life outside of the office. If you have practiced good time management skills in your work and still cannot get your work completed, talk to your supervisor about other solutions. Remember, if you don't have a balanced personal and professional life, both parts of your life will suffer.

Stay in Control

Managing your time is really a matter of staying in control. If you don't control your time, someone else, or the whims of the world, will. Your success in business will be a direct reflection of the extent to which you control your time.

QUICK RECAP 2.2

MANAGING YOUR TIME

- By managing your time, you can be an effective and efficient professional.
- Avoid procrastination by starting or planning a project. Avoid distractions and take at least the first step to start the project.
- Develop good work habits by focusing, planning, communicating, sticking to tasks, and working carefully and methodically.
- Use lists and timetables to plan your work.
- Planning will help you work more efficiently.
- Multitask when one task is inactive or requires no thought or action.
- Control meetings by sticking to an agenda and directing input from others.

CHECK YOURSELF

1. What is the best way to stop a bad habit?
2. List the kinds of information you should include in a plan.

Check you answers online at **www.mhhe.com/pace.**

BUSINESS VOCABULARY

contingency   an alternate plan to be used if things go wrong
delegating   assigning a project, responsibility, or authority to someone else
effectiveness   the extent to which efforts produce expected results
efficiency   the ratio of input to output; that is, the amount of energy that is put into the production of something compared to the quantity actually produced
multitasking   the activity of working on more than one task at a time
prioritize   rate the importance of a task
procrastination   the act of putting off until later what you should do now

Managing Your Stress

Stress! It's as much a part of American business as telephones and computers. Despite the number of high-tech, labor-saving devices, everyone is working harder and faster, cranking out work as never before. This is good for profits and productivity, but it comes at a cost called stress. Stress isn't just jangled nerves. It's the cause of many physical illnesses and many a sleepless night. It's also an obstacle to success because no one under the crush of stress can perform a job well.

Manage Stress. You can keep stress under control. You can identify where it comes from, deal with it when it happens, use a little of it to keep yourself challenged, and put the rest of it to sleep while you do your job and live your life. In this section, we'll look at some of the ways to manage stress.

Managing Stress

Stress happens. It happens when the work pile gets too deep, when the boss snaps at you, when you have to speak before a group of strangers, when you have to work extra hours, when you have to be in two places at once, and when you're torn between the needs of your family and your job.

Unless you have plans for a profession in a Tibetan monastery, stress is going to happen to you. If you accept and use a certain level of stress, the results can be beneficial. But if the stress gets to be too much, it can literally kill you. At the very least, it can leave you confused, agitated, ineffective, inefficient, and spinning your professional wheels. That, of course, just adds to your stress.

The Signs of Stress

Stress is an uncomfortable and disruptive mental or emotional state brought on by an outside influence. Some of the symptoms are well known.

- **Physical symptoms** include headaches, insomnia (sleeplessness), daytime sleepiness and fatigue, backaches, clenched jaw, constipation, diarrhea, rash, strange aches and pains, clumsiness, high blood pressure, heart attack, and possibly other illnesses, from colds to cancer.
- **Emotional symptoms** include anxiety, depression, mood swings, irritability, nervousness, low self-esteem, anger, aggression, and inability to laugh or relax.
- **Mental symptoms** include memory loss and forgetfulness, confusion, trouble concentrating, carelessness, inability to decide simple matters, and a tendency to daydream, all of which adds up to a drop in productivity and an increase in mistakes.
- **Social symptoms** include distrust of others, blaming of others for problems, defensiveness, and inability to get along with others.

Reading and Study Tip

Character
Look at the characters used to illustrate ideas in this section. Think about their names, their personalities, and their situations. How does using characters help illustrate examples of stress? On a separate sheet of paper, make up your own character to illustrate one idea in the text.

---

stress an uncomfortable and disruptive mental or emotional state brought on by an outside influence

Worry a little bit every day and in a lifetime you will lose a couple of years. If something is wrong, fix it if you can. But train yourself not to worry. Worry never fixes anything.

Mary Hemingway
Author

Sources of Stress

Stress can come from a great number of sources. Sometimes they are easy to spot. Other times, you may not realize how much something is affecting you. Stress sources can be categorized into four groups: change, threat, internal, and environmental.

Change A recent marriage, divorce, death, birth, move to a new home, new job, new project assignment, trip, new boss, new problem, new work shift—all of these can cause stress. Even if it is a good change, it can cause stress.

Threat Threats can include competition in your office or the marketplace, the possibility of losing a job for any reason, an ultimatum from the boss, threat of divorce, a letter from the Internal Revenue Service, fear of failure, and so on. Excess work could be included here, too, as it threatens you with failure, criticism, or even real disaster.

Internal Much stress is generated by nothing more than the mind as it presumes that the worst will happen, that all problems and threats are extreme. Your mind may tell you that you are not capable of doing something, that your personal situation is exceptionally bad and far worse than you deserve, that nothing ever works for you, and so on. Internal stress also can be caused by lack of sleep and such abuses as alcohol, cigarettes, and drugs. Internal stress also might include difficulties in getting things organized and preparing for future tasks and projects.

Environmental You can be stressed by conditions around you, such as constant noise, aggressive behavior in others, interruptions, real dangers, chaos, other stressed people, and extremes of heat, cold, humidity, and so forth.

Stress Causes Stress

Stress tends to cause the same kinds of problems that cause stress. For example, you can get too stressed to stop and organize your life. The disorganization causes you to forget things and sleep poorly. These factors cause you to make mistakes, which increases your stress level, which makes it even harder for you to get organized and sleep well. See Figure 2.4.

Reducing Stress

Most stress can be reduced or eliminated by identifying its source and dealing with it. Sometimes the simple act of recognizing the source of stress can take much of the pressure off of you. Usually you can easily identify the source of your stress.

Dealing with Change

Change is inevitable, and life would be terribly dull without it. Every life faces occasional big changes.

- Acknowledge that things are changing or going to change. Change is not a terminal crisis. It is a challenge that you can and must confront. Accept the change.
- When you see change coming, sit down and calmly plan the best way to handle it.
- When change happens unexpectedly, sit down and calmly plan the best way to handle it.
- Things that remain stable during change may be like life preservers. Hold on to them and appreciate them during the change.

Figure 2.4 *The Cycle of Stress*

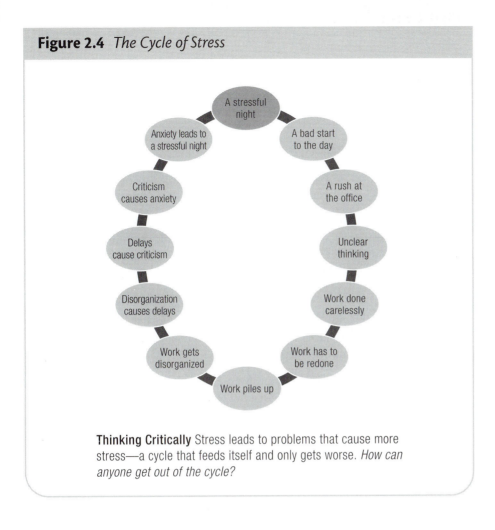

Thinking Critically Stress leads to problems that cause more stress—a cycle that feeds itself and only gets worse. *How can anyone get out of the cycle?*

- Appreciate change as a challenge, not a disaster. You will survive it.
- Remember that change always creates opportunity.

Feeling Threatened

Threat is an unfortunate but inevitable part of life. However, threats are rarely as serious as they seem. It's usually best to confront them with either questions or resistance.

- If you sense threat from someone who should be an ally, talk with the person openly and honestly to understand what's happening. It may be that you misread someone who simply has a different personality style.
- When you are threatened by a competitor (that is, threatened in the business sense of being faced with tough competition), meet with your team to devise a competitive response.
- Assess perceived threats. Are they real? How serious are they?

Dealing with Internal Stress

All stress, really, is internal because something outside of you triggers a stressed reaction inside of you. The release of that stress, too, must come from inside you.

- Assess yourself for personal causes of stress, such as lack of sleep, chemical abuses, poor diet, no exercise, turbulent life, lack of organization, and so forth. Solve these problems even if they don't seem related to your stress.

Dr. Joe Pace
ATTITUDE

" Keep your face to the sunshine and you cannot see the shadows."

- Assess the seriousness of external causes of stress and bring internal stress into an appropriate balance.
- Learn to meditate. Even at your desk, on a plane, or in a waiting room, sit in a comfortable position, relax every muscle you can find, and concentrate on your breathing, focusing on each inhalation and exhalation.
- Consider psychotherapy as a potential tune-up of the maturing mind.

Environmental Stress

You have a right to a safe working environment. If the noise, temperature, interruptions, threats, or postures of your workplace are causing stress, they are truly a health hazard.

- If possible, eliminate the cause of the stress.
- Counteract the source. That may mean using earplugs for noise or wearing layers for a cold office.
- Talk with management about the problem. Work with them to find a solution.

Get Organized

❝ *A day of worry is more exhausting than a week of work.* **❞**

John Lubbock
Nineteenth-Century British Banker and Statesman

You can probably relieve a lot of stress by getting yourself, your life, and your work organized. Much of this book is dedicated to exactly that.

- Set reasonable goals and plan how to reach them.
- Manage your time.
- Organize the details of your life—your date book, your list of addresses and phone numbers, your checkbook, your e-mail, your files, your travel arrangements, your laundry, everything. Then keep it organized.
- Do one thing at a time. Finish it. File it. Only then should you start the next thing.
- Admit what you can't change and whom you can't please.
- Limit your workload.

QUICK RECAP 2.3

MANAGING YOUR STRESS

- Stress is normal, but it must be controlled.
- Symptoms of stress can be physical, mental, emotional, and social.
- Stress can be caused by change, threats, internal sources, and environmental factors.
- Stress itself can cause the same kinds of problems that cause stress.
- In most cases, you can reduce stress by identifying the source, then confronting it.

CHECK YOURSELF

1. How can stress be a cause of stress?
2. What are some techniques for reducing stress caused by unexpected changes in your life?

Check you answers online at: www.mhhe.com/pace.

Pace
ONLINE

BUSINESS VOCABULARY

stress   an uncomfortable and disruptive mental or emotional state brought on by an outside influence

Managing Your Money

Money isn't everything, but it's a big part of life. Well-managed money can give you the peace of mind that you need to get other things done. Well-managed money can provide you with more than your salary alone could buy. Learn how to invest well, how to protect yourself from being overtaxed, and how to avoid high interest payments. Your money can lead you and your family to a comfortable future and a timely retirement. In effect, it can buy you time.

Money Management. Don't just work for your money. Make your money work for you! Be smart about how you spend and invest it. Find that balance between living well and preparing to live well. It's a matter of planning. This section should help you learn how.

Your Financial Philosophy

Finance is the science of managing money and other **assets,** such as your house, jewelry, computer, and other things that have value. You started practicing finance as soon as you started making money for yourself. The practice of finance ranges from the setting of a family's budget to the management of a corporation's billions of dollars.

To be at peak performance at work, you need to have your financial life in order. Smart financial management is an important part of your overall personal success. Your financial strategies will probably include the following principles:

- Spend less than you earn.
- Use debt to increase your wealth.
- Avoid high-interest debt.
- Use a budget.
- Invest in yourself.
- Invest in your family.
- Invest in your future finances.

Spend Less Than You Earn

This principle is not as obvious as it seems. Yes, you should avoid buying things that you can't pay for. But in a few cases, such as buying a house or a car or paying tuition, you will probably need to borrow money. Still, the principle remains: your monthly payments should not be more than you can afford.

Use Debt to Increase Your Wealth

If you're careful and smart, you can use short-term debt to increase long-term wealth. A mortgage is a debt of as much as 30 years, but it allows you to buy a house that should increase in value. A **home equity loan**—a loan secured by the value of your house—that is wisely invested can gain more wealth than the value of the loan. A **business loan**—a loan to start or expand a business—can help you start a business that brings in income for you.

Reading and Study Tip

Numbers
Numbers can be written out in words or as numerical symbols. When using numbers in writing, the numbers one through ten should be written out, while higher numbers can be written as symbols such as 11, 12, 13. Similarly, "dollars" can be written out or can be represented using the $ sign. Look at how numbers are written in this section. On a separate sheet of paper write out in words these numbers: 27; 150; 6,532; 14.

finance the science of managing money and other assets

assets things that have value, such as a house, stocks and bonds, and a car

home equity loan a loan secured by the value of your house

business loan a loan to start or expand a business

Internet Quest

Interesting Interest

Use a search engine to find information on different credit card offers. Find the interest rates for one. Use a calculator to figure out what the interest rate would be on a $500.00 purchase that is overdue by one month, six months, and one year. Look at the difference in the amount borrowed and the amount owed in interest after a year.

> *If you would be wealthy, think of saving as well as getting.*
>
> **Benjamin Franklin**
> *Eighteenth-Century Writer, Scientist, Inventor, and Politician*

> *A wise man should have money in his head, but not in his heart.*
>
> **Jonathan Swift**
> *Eighteenth-Century Irish Author and Humorist*

budget a set amount of money to spend on different categories of expenses

cash flow projection an estimate of how much you will earn and how much you will spend

Avoid High-Interest Debt

Loans for cars and houses usually have a low interest rate. Interest on credit card debt, however, is often two or three times higher. When credit card debt amounts to thousands of dollars, the monthly interest rate can become a real burden. When you calculate how much you spent to buy an item and include how much you paid in interest, you may have ended up paying much more for an item than it was ever worth. Credit cards are easy to use, but they may be hard to pay off!

Use a Budget

Devise a written budget. It should show your total income and all your expenses, such as rent, car payments, food, insurance, and so on. One part of that budget should include adding to your savings or investments.

Invest in Yourself

Money invested in your money-earning capabilities is money well invested. Among these investments are tuition for school, health care, and the clothes you need to look professional. A nice car stereo, however, isn't an investment in yourself. Nor are an excessive number of shoes, an extravagant vacation, or other luxuries, if you can't afford them.

Invest in Your Family

Part of your responsibility as a human being, citizen, spouse, and parent is to invest in your family. You need a decent place to live. You all need to stay healthy. Your children need to go to school. Investment in family demands spending in the present and planning for the future.

Invest in Your Future Finances

You need to invest now to have money for college tuition in the future. You also will need to retire someday. Money invested early in your life will build tremendously over the course of decades. Small sacrifices today can save you from financial difficulties in the future.

How Are They Doing?

Bonnie takes her finances seriously, and little by little, her life gets better. Dave is more laid-back, taking one day at a time, as his financial problems build and cause problems that worsen his situation. Find where each person is on the steps to good finances in Figure 2.5.

Your Budget

You will need to set and stick to budgets for your personal life as well as for your job. In both cases, the principles are the same. A **budget** is a set amount of money to spend on different categories of expenses. Your budget depends on your **cash flow projection,** that is, your estimates of how much you will earn and how much you will spend.

Figure 2.5 *Steps to Good Finances*

If You Do This:	You Can Avoid This:	And Accomplish This:
Spend less than you earn	Falling into debt and paying interest	Investing steadily and earning interest
Borrow at low interest for an investment, such as a house	Paying rent and not having an asset that increases in value	Seeing the value of your investment rise faster than the interest rate you're paying
Don't overspend on your credit card	Paying painfully high interest rates	Using extra cash for investment rather than credit card interest
Use a budget	Spending more than you earn	Keeping your expenses in line with your income
Invest in yourself with education	Slower career advancement	Faster career advancement and better pay
Invest in your family	Family problems that hurt the ones you love and complicate your life	Seeing the ones you love live satisfying lives
Invest in your future	A late retirement (or no retirement at all)	Retirement at a comfortable age and a life of financial security
Use insurance to manage risk	Financial disaster due to an accident or another unexpected crisis	Using low, regular payments to avoid the need for huge and devastating payments at a difficult time
Invest in 401(k) plans and IRA accounts	Paying income tax on all your earnings	Avoiding some income taxes until you retire and your tax rate is lower
Pay bills on time and stay out of excessive debt	Going bankrupt	Keep a good financial track record that helps you borrow money and use credit cards
Pay all necessary taxes	Legal problems and even the loss of property	Know that you are contributing to government services

Thinking Critically If you follow the steps to good finances, you can avoid much stress and hardship. *What step can you choose to follow now?*

Set up a chart as shown in Figure 2.6 (page 54):

1. Determine your **revenues**—that, is, all your income, including tips, commissions, gifts of money, interest, and so forth.
2. Determine your necessary expenses—your mortgage or rent, insurance policies, and payments on credit, transportation, child care, food, taxes, and so on.
3. Determine occasional necessary expenses—clothing, household supplies, and so forth.
4. Determine an amount for other expenses—entertainment, furniture, miscellaneous.
5. Determine savings/investment commitment—regular contributions to an investment plan such as a 401(k).

The projected expenses are your budget. Ideally, your revenues will equal your expenses. You will have to take whatever steps are necessary to ensure that your total expenses are not more than your total revenues.

revenues all your income, including tips, commissions, gifts of money, and interest

Figure 2.6 *Monthly Budget*

	Month 1		Month 2		Month 3	
	Estimated	*Actual*	*Estimated*	*Actual*	*Estimated*	*Actual*
Revenues						
• Salary						
• Commissions						
• Other income						
• Total revenues						
Expenses						
• Mortgage or rent						
• Car loan payments and other expenses						
• Food						
• Insurance						
• Clothing						
• Taxes						
• Credit card interest						
• Savings/investment						
• Etc.						
• Etc.						
• Total payments						
Revenues minus expenses						

Thinking Critically For each month, note how much you estimate you will earn and spend, and then how much you actually earn and spend. *Compare your total revenues and expenses. Are they about equal? What numbers should you compare at the end of each month?*

Investment

portfolio a set of investments

People invest for two main reasons: to save for retirement and to protect their earnings from taxes. A financial planner can help you develop an investment **portfolio,** that is, a set of investments. The kinds of investments you make should be planned carefully, so that the overall investment is as secure as possible while earning the highest interest possible. Everyone who earns income should take advantage of two investment programs—401(k) plans and IRA accounts.

stock rights to having partial ownership of a company

Stocks When you buy **stock,** you buy partial ownership of a company. When the company makes a profit, it often gives dividends (portions of the profit) to its stockholders. When companies are profitable, the value of their stock often rises.

bond company's or government's promise to pay back a sum of money plus interest over time

Bonds When you buy **bonds,** you are buying a company's or a government's promise to pay back the money plus interest over time. It is like the company is getting a loan from you. When you buy government bonds, you don't have to pay taxes on the interest you earn.

mutual fund a portfolio of both stock and bond investments

Mutual Funds A **mutual fund** is a portfolio of both stock and bond investments. Because mutual funds offer a variety of types of stocks and bonds, your investment values will generally rise and fall along with the general stock market.

401(k) Plans If your company offers a 401(k) plan, you can invest part of your salary in whatever options your company offers. The company will match your investment, so you've already doubled your money. The amount that you invest is not taxable until you withdraw it after retirement.

IRA Accounts Everyone who works can invest a certain amount in an independent retirement account. IRA accounts are usually set up by banks and financial brokers (companies that specialize in selling investment plans). The amount you invest is not taxable until you withdraw it. Since you'll probably be earning less after retirement, your taxes on this money will be lower. You can invest IRA contributions many ways.

Credit Cards

Credit cards are almost a necessity in modern life, and you may well need them for your job. Many hotels and car rental companies require a credit card. Credit cards are also a good way to keep track of your expenses.

But as you know, credit cards often charge extremely high interest rates if you fail to pay off your debt at the end of the month. Avoid credit card debt.

- Use credit cards that have a low interest rate. Read the small print in the agreement. Some charge a low rate for a few months, then increase it.
- Use one credit card for business, another for personal expenses.
- If you can't pay off your credit card debt, stop using all credit cards except as necessary for business.
- If possible, find a loan at a lower interest rate—a home equity loan, for example—and use it to pay off credit card debt.

> *Never spend your money before you have it.*
>
> Thomas Jefferson
> *Third President of the United States*

Bankruptcy

Bankruptcy is the legal situation in which you admit that you cannot pay all of your debts on time. Usually you will be required to reschedule your debts, that is, pay them off at a slower rate. You may have to sell some of your assets, such as a house or car.

Bankruptcy is not an easy way out of paying debts. Not only will you probably have to pay all the debts, but you will add legal expenses to your debt. The biggest drawback is that you will have bad credit. You will not be able to borrow money for many years—no mortgage, no car loans, no credit cards, no student loans. You may not be able to hold certain jobs. You will be at a personal and professional disadvantage for many years.

bankruptcy the legal situation in which you admit that you cannot pay all of your debts on time

Insurance to Manage Risk

Insurance is used to manage risk by helping to pay for unexpected occurrences, such as accidents, health problems, and other emergencies. People use insurance to prevent total financial disaster. By paying for insurance policies, they protect themselves from serious financial problems. Many insurance policies require a deductible: the amount that you must pay before the insurance company pays the expenses of your accident or problem.

You would be foolish not to have some kind of insurance for you and your family's health, cars, house, and lives. The people who provide income for your family—you and possibly your spouse—need enough life insurance to provide income for the rest of the family for many years.

Insurance can be very complicated. You will need an insurance agent to offer suitable and affordable policies. Consult at least two agents before you make a decision.

Taxes

Federal, state, and local governments collect taxes to raise money for schools, police protection, the justice system, national defense, social programs, and all the other services that governments provide. Taxes are a necessary part of living in modern society. You will have to pay several kinds of taxes.

Income Tax   The federal government taxes each citizen based on a percentage of the money earned. Your employer will probably deduct your **income tax** from your paycheck before you receive it. If you are self-employed, you will have to estimate your yearly income and pay an estimated tax every three months. Income tax can be a little difficult to figure out, so you should consider hiring a tax preparer to help you.

income tax a tax based on a percentage of money earned

State Taxes   These vary from state to state. Some states have income taxes, others have sales tax, some have both, and some have neither. If there is an income tax in your state, you will need to file a tax return.

Municipal Taxes   Local governments usually tax you based on the value of your property, such as real estate and cars. You will probably receive bills for these taxes, though real estate taxes are often included with mortgage payments. If you fail to pay municipal taxes, your town government may be able to take your property and sell it to pay the taxes.

Taxes and Your Paycheck

When you receive a paycheck from your employer, you'll notice that a large amount has been subtracted for taxes. The check should come with information that explains where this money went. Typically, some (roughly 25 percent, depending on your income level) goes to federal income tax. About 7.5 percent goes to your Social Security account—your contribution to money you will receive when you retire or become disabled. A certain percentage may go to a state income tax.

When you file your tax returns, you may receive some of this money back. If enough hasn't been deducted, you also may also be required to pay more. If there are no taxes deducted from your paycheck, you may be required to make these payments yourself. Check with your employer or a tax consultant.

QUICK RECAP 2.4

MANAGING YOUR MONEY

- By keeping your financial life in order, you'll be better able to fully dedicate your mind to your job.
- To remain financially secure, spend less than you earn, borrow money only for necessities and investments, follow a written budget, and invest in yourself, your family, and your future.
- Avoid high-interest credit card debt.
- A monthly budget chart will help you keep track of your income and spending.
- Investments in 401(k) plans and IRA accounts minimize your taxes while helping you prepare for your future.
- Bankruptcy can limit your opportunities for years to come.
- Insurance helps minimize the risk of major financial disaster.
- Federal, state, and municipal taxes help pay for government services.

CHECK YOURSELF

1. What are some disadvantages to declaring bankruptcy?
2. What kinds of things should you list on your monthly budget chart?

Check your answers online at **www.mhhe.com/pace.** *Pace* ONLINE

BUSINESS VOCABULARY

assets   things that have value, such as a house, stocks and bonds, and a car

bankruptcy   the legal situation in which you admit that you cannot pay all of your debts on time

bond   a company's or government's promise to pay back a sum of money plus interest over time

budget   a set amount of money to spend on different categories of expenses

business loan   a loan to start or expand a business

cash flow projection   an estimate of how much you will earn and how much you will spend

finance   the science of managing money and other assets

home equity loan   a loan secured by the value of your house

income tax   a tax based on a percentage of money earned

mutual fund   a portfolio of both stock and bond investments

portfolio   a set of investments

revenues   all your income, including tips, commissions, gifts of money, and interest

stock   rights to having partial ownership of a company

Managing Yourself

In this book, you've learned to set and reach goals, to use your attitude to get ahead, and to manage your time, stress, and finances. These are the big elements of professional and personal success. Now we need to discuss just one more thing, the one that counts the most—you.

Build a Better You.   You have within you all the basic elements of success. You already know a lot, and you're ready to learn more. You have your goals, and you want to succeed. You can do it, but it will take effort. You will need to constantly change and grow in a positive direction.

Reading and Study Tip

The First Person
This section talks about self-management. "You" is used to address a second person or persons directly. Notice how you are being addressed directly throughout the book. Choose one paragraph and, on a separate sheet of paper, rewrite it in the first person singular using *me*, *myself*, and *I*.

Managing Yourself

You are reaching a very important new stage in your life. That's why you're reading this book and thinking about how to succeed in your professional and personal life. This should be very exciting for you. You are ready to become a better person and a better professional.

In other words, you are going to have to make a **transition**—a change from one stage of development to another. To make this transition, you will need to manage yourself almost as if you were a company that must be run efficiently in order to succeed. Just as a company cannot succeed if its employees waste time or lack focus, you yourself cannot succeed if you are not focused, directed, competent, and dynamic.

Pulling It All Together

As you may have noticed, managing yourself is a complicated business. It involves a lot of activities: planning, deciding, improving, changing, and so on. If you try to juggle all of this in your head, you're bound to lose track of something, and your best intentions may collapse into chaos.

So, start a personal management notebook. Here you will keep track of your self-improvement plans and review your progress over time. There are a number of areas you will want to put on paper. Note that in each area, the emphasis is on how to make a positive change in your life. Of course, your personal management notebook will need to keep changing during your entire career . . . as will you.

> " Everyone has inside of him a piece of good news. The good news is that you don't know how great you can be! How much you can love! What you can accomplish! And what your potential is! "
>
> *Anne Frank*
> *Dutch Writer and Holocaust Victim*

transition a change from one stage of development to another

New Attitudes / New Opportunities

Meet Paulo Pisano. Paulo is originally from Brazil and currently lives in New York City, working in Corporate Human Resources for Citigroup. Paulo's job includes coaching managers, employees, and other clients. As a coach, he helps people become more effective and satisfied in their jobs and lives. He encourages clients to solve their own problems by helping them examine their habits and patterns of behavior. Here's what Paulo had to say about . . .

How Coaching Can Help People Identify What Is Causing Their Problems "The idea of coaching is distinct from consulting or counseling, where you give answers to a person. We don't provide answers to the person we are coaching; we help them observe their own situation. We want them to become aware of how they act or react. Then, as they look at that situation from a different perspective, they can find different solutions. We believe that people have the solutions for their own problems, but they are stuck somehow."

Important Steps to Improving Habits "First of all, it's important to become aware of the situation. Then you can work backwards. Ask yourself, 'This is too tough, but *why* is it? How is it that I got here to begin with? Were things always like this?' The other thing to think about is priorities. We help people list the important and urgent things in their lives. Typically, people focus a lot on the urgent—but not necessarily important—things. Knowing how you build priorities for yourself is important for better time management."

How to Implement Changes "No one changes overnight. I think making these changes is a step-by-step process. It's important to know where you want to get to, to know what you should change. It's important to have a vision of where you want to be, so you can always look at that as a baseline or a benchmark. Then you know which direction to go."

How Being Aware of Our Reactions Can Help Us Manage Stress "You need to be aware of your internal dialogue, what you tell yourself in certain situations. If you can catch yourself telling yourself something that creates stress, it's already the first step towards dealing with it. If I'm in a dark subway with a large group up ahead, and I start thinking to myself, 'Oh no, what if they're going to mug me, or what if . . .,' that language is what starts generating stress. It's the same at work, 'Oh no, there's a deadline coming up! Can I make it?' Watch what you tell yourself in a situation and explore a positive outcome or a positive alternative. This changes your dialogue; and stress doesn't build up the same way."

Stress-Busting Moments "If you have a busy day, plan a few times where you can find a quiet place to sit down for five minutes without doing anything. Just close your eyes, breathe, and relax. It's like if you carry a weight with your right arm until it's exhausted, and you change to the left arm until it's exhausted, at the end of the day you have two exhausted arms. However, if you switch arms before they tire out, you last much longer. It's the same principle. Sometimes people wait until the end of the day to go to the gym to unwind, but a little rest throughout the day can do as much to help the stress."

Short-Term Goals

Get a B or above in all of my
courses this term

My plan:

- Commit to 2 hours of studying after
  dinner each night

- Cut back on television one hour
  each night

- Join a study group one night a week

Long-Term Goals

Find employment in retail sales

My plan:

- Visit local retailers for part-time job
  or internship

- Ask my career services office for an
  alumni mentor to advise me

---

*" Don't lower your
expectations to meet your
performance. Raise your
level of performance to
meet your expectations.
Expect the best of
yourself, and then do
what is necessary to
make it a reality. "*

Ralph Marston
Author of The Daily Motivator

Short-Term and Long-Term Goals   Write your goals down on paper.

- Detail the steps needed to reach each goal.
- Identify obstacles you expect in the future. Explore ideas for overcoming them.
- Identify ways that you must change in order to meet each goal.

Lay Out Short-Term and Long-Term Timetables   Plan out timetables for your various goals and projects.

- One timetable should be for the rest of your life. (Obviously, it will be a little vague and subject to change.)
- The shortest timetable may cover as little as a week, or even less.
- Your timetable may include changes that you want to make in yourself.

Identify Skills   Keep an inventory of your skills.

- List the skills that you have.
- List the skills that you need to acquire.
- For each skill that you have, note (a) how to improve it and (b) how to avoid losing it.
- For each skill you need, note (a) where and how you can acquire it and (b) when you can begin to acquire it.

Patterns of Behavior   As you change your patterns of behavior, you become better able to succeed in your profession.

- List the patterns of behavior in your life (your habits and lifestyle) that will help or hinder you in your professional pursuits.

- For each thing that will hinder you, note realistic ways that you can change the pattern.
- Write a plan for changing each of those negative patterns into positive patterns.

Increased Productivity   Professional success is a matter of productivity: the ability to get things done.

- List ways that you can become more productive, such as starting work earlier, focusing on tasks, and planning better.
- List obstacles to your productivity, be it personal habits, lack of know-how, other people, and so on.
- Write plans for removing those obstacles.

People   Other people can make or break you. You need to handle relationships appropriately.

- List people who help you and note how they help.
- Identify a mentor or two, if you have any, noting how they help and how you can let them help more. If you have no real mentors, identify people who might serve as such if you asked them for help. Consider how to approach them.
- Think about how you can help all of the people who are helping you.
- List people who are obstacles to your progress and productivity, noting (a) how they are holding you back and (b) how you can resolve the problem.

Personal Fitness   Is your personal fitness going to help or hinder your professional ambition?

- Assess your program of exercise. Are you sticking with it?
- If your exercise is inadequate, write a plan for getting in shape.
- Monitor your progress daily until exercise becomes a habit.
- Note any health issues that you should discuss with a doctor.
- List ways that you can look more professional, such as better grooming and nicer clothes.

Advice   Good advice is as good as gold. But sometimes advice is painful and hard to take.

- Note advice you have received, and note whether you think it was good or bad advice.
- In cases of seemingly good advice that you have not taken, identify the reason and consider how you can change that.
- In cases of seemingly bad advice, reconsider whether maybe it's advice that's really good but too hard to take.

> *Doing the best at this moment puts you in the best place for the next moment.*
>
> *Oprah Winfrey*
> *Talk-show Host and Businesswoman*

Build a Better You

There is no project more valuable than building a better you. Consistently improving yourself can only lead to a more satisfying life and more successful career. It doesn't happen easily or automatically, but it's worth every bit of effort.

Tips From a Mentor

Ten Things to Do with Advice

- **Thank the advisor.** Whether or not you agree with the advice, the person giving it at least thinks that he or she is saying it for your own good. Accept the good wishes.

- **Don't take it personally.** Take any criticism as a comment about an action of yours, not about you as a person. Feeling defensive will not help you in any way.

- **Think about the advice.** Try to look at the situation objectively and decide if you should take all, some, or none of the advice.

- **Write it down** for future consideration. You may be too shocked or hurt to look at the situation objectively at first. Or perhaps you are working on larger, more important issues in your life. Save the advice for later.

- **Ask for a second opinion** from a different person. Choose someone you respect or someone who knows you well—preferably both.

- **Request more information** or specific details. If you don't understand or you disagree, the person giving advice should be able to clear up any misunderstanding by giving specific examples.

- **Try taking the advice.** Follow the advice given for a certain amount of time.

- **Ask for a solution.** Sometimes others will tell us what *not* to do. Ask them what he or she thinks you *should* do instead. You may even ask for their help in following the advice.

- **Disregard it.** After you have thanked the advice-giver and thought about his or her advice, do what you think is best. That may mean forgetting all about what was said.

- **Follow-up.** If the advice yielded good results, let the person who gave it to you know.

QUICK RECAP 2.5

MANAGING YOURSELF

- As you go into the business world, you will need to become a better person and a better professional.
- A personal management notebook will help you identify ways to make a positive change in your professional life.
- As you set goals, identify ways that you must change in order to reach them.
- Your skills inventory should include the skills you need to acquire.
- As you change your patterns of behavior, you become better able to succeed in your profession.

- Professional success is a matter of productivity.
- People can help or hinder your efforts to succeed.
- Good advice is valuable, but it can be painful to accept.
- Personal fitness can fuel your professional progress.

CHECK YOURSELF

1. Why does a professional need to change in order to succeed in a career?
2. How can a professional become more productive?

Check you answers online at www.mhhe.com/pace.

BUSINESS VOCABULARY

transition   a change from one stage of development to another

Chapter Summary

2.1 Assessing Your Lifestyle

Objective: *Identify aspects of your lifestyle that work for or against your career.*

In this section, you learned the importance of stepping back from yourself to assess your lifestyle and patterns of behavior. Your personal habits and the general way you communicate with others, organize your life and finances, dedicate yourself to continuous learning, and discipline yourself all add up to your overall capability as a professional.

2.2 Managing Your Time

Objective: *Use your time wisely and productively.*

You should manage your time, not let time manage you. In this section, you learned how to make yourself more efficient and effective by avoiding bad work habits, keeping your activities organized, avoiding procrastination, and avoiding distractions. You saw the importance of prioritizing your activities, delegating tasks to others, communicating with team members, multitasking, and staying focused.

2.3 Managing Your Stress

Objective: *Control your stress level by understanding what causes stress.*

In this section, you learned about stress: where it comes from, what it can do to you, and how to manage it by minimizing it.

Change can be a major source of stress, so you considered a few ways to cope with changes. You saw how stress can come from inside you. Lack of organization at home and at the office can cause more stress and result in more disorganization.

2.4 Managing Your Money

Objective: *Keep your finances in order and put your money to good use.*

In this section, you learned how well-managed finances can give you the peace of mind that you need to get other things done. You saw how a budget and cash flow projection can help you spend less than you earn. Investing in yourself and your family are an important part of managing your money.

2.5 Managing Yourself

Objective: *Make strategic changes in your life in order to become more productive and more satisfied.*

In this section, you recognized that by managing yourself, you make yourself a better person and better professional. Self-management demands the setting of goals, the identification and development of skills, the disciplined control of habits, the drive to increase productivity, the recognition of who can help you or hold you back, the consideration of good advice, and the maintenance of physical fitness.

Business Vocabulary

- assets (p. 51)
- bankruptcy (p. 55)
- bond (p. 54)
- budget (p. 52)
- business loan (p. 51)
- cash flow projection (p. 52)
- contingency (p. 42)
- delegating (p. 42)
- effectiveness (p. 41)
- efficiency (p. 40)
- finance (p. 51)
- home equity loan (p. 51)
- income tax (p. 56)
- mentor (p. 38)
- multitasking (p. 44)
- mutual fund (p. 54)
- patterns of behavior (p. 36)
- portfolio (p. 54)
- prioritize (p. 42)
- procrastination (p. 41)
- revenues (p. 53)
- stock (p. 54)
- stress (p. 47)
- transition (p. 58)

Key Concepts Review

1. Give five examples of patterns of behavior that would help a professional succeed. (2.1)

2. How can a mentor help a professional when he or she is just starting? (2.1)

3. What is the difference between efficiency and effectiveness? (2.2)

4. What are the major obstacles to efficiency and effectiveness? (2.2)

5. List several physical and mental symptoms of stress. (2.3)

6. How can stress cause stress? (2.3)

7. What is finance ? (2.4)

8. What is the difference between a budget and a cash flow projection? (2.4)

9. What kind of transition do you need to make as you enter the business world? (2.5)

10. How can you increase your productivity in order to become a better professional? (2.5)

Online Project

Take Care of Yourself

Use a search engine to find different sources of a few printed publications (books, government manuals, trade association pamphlets, etc.) that would teach you about each of the following areas: (a) general self-improvement, (b) managing personal finances, (c) reducing stress, and (d) managing time.

Step Up the *Pace*

CASE A   *Help a Friend Improve*

A good friend of yours has just graduated from college. He's been out for four months but has made no progress toward getting a job. You can imagine why. He's a slob. He sleeps late. He could be a professional procrastinator. He spends half the day on the phone, yakking with his mother. He gets depressed over how much he owes on his credit cards, yet he never bothers to balance his checkbook. His idea of exercise is opening beer cans and surfing TV channels. But he's a good guy, and he recognizes the success that you have made of yourself. In total despair, he asks you for help.

What to Do

1. Outline an assessment of his lifestyle and patterns of behavior. Cover every part of his life. (Make up a few things if you need to.)
2. Start a personal management notebook for your friend, beginning pages with the kinds of things he needs to manage.

CASE B   *Reduce a Co-worker's Stress*

Your co-worker at a small, but busy, public relations agency is on the verge of a nervous breakdown. She's an excellent worker, at least in terms of energy. She puts in 12 hours a day, yet her desk is always piled high with unfinished projects, some of which shouldn't even be hers. Desperate to catch up and terrified of getting fired, she's always doing three things at once, though she never seems to finish any of them. She's pale, is putting on weight, has bags under her eyes, and she's has been snapping at you and others for no reason. She needs help before she cracks up or does indeed get fired.

What to Do

1. Outline a stress reduction program for your friend, covering every area where you perceive a need for her to change her behavior.
2. Think of any ways that her stress and yours (in your real life) are similar. What could the two of you do together to reduce your stress and do a better job?

Rounding

In business and in life, rounding is a handy skill to have. *Rounding* means adjusting a figure to its nearest whole number, such as rounding $7.52 to $8.00.

Follow these steps for better rounding skills:

1. Determine a place value to round to. For example, you may choose to round to the nearest dollar when estimating how much something costs. If you're buying a house though, you would probably round to the nearest $10,000. If you're buying concert tickets, you might round to the nearest $10.
2. Use the number in the place you want to round to and the number in the place to the right of it. For example, if you want to round 3.76 to the nearest 1, look at only the 3 and the 7 (it rounds up to 4). If you want to round 314 to the nearest 10, look at the 1 and the 4 (it rounds down to 310).
3. Round down to the next lower number if the place is 1–4. For example, 14 rounds down to 10.
4. Round up to the next number if the place is 5–9. For example, 3.7 rounds up to 4.
5. If the number is 0, don't change it.

Draw a line to match each number to its rounded number.

A) 29	**1)** 20
B) 20	**2)** 20
C) 24	**3)** 30
D) 32	**4)** 30
E) 35	**5)** 40

Both A and D become 30. Both B and C round to 20. Finally, E becomes 40.

Exercise: Round each number below.

54
16
97
$3.75
33%
4.2
8.0
2,611
809
0.7

Exercise: Round each number below to the place indicated. The first one is done for you.

Round This Number to the . . .	Nearest 1	Nearest 10	Nearest 100
13.5	14	10	0
19			
204			
388.9			
42			
51.3			

Communicate with Confidence

What Will You Do?

3.1 Communicating in Writing Learn the importance of writing clearly, simply, and logically.

3.2 Thinking Critically and Creatively Understand that critical thinking calls for a logical, methodical approach to a problem, while creative thinking looks for inspiration in unexpected places.

3.3 Developing Your Vocabulary See how words can be powerful tools, understand the different types of words used in business, and look at ways to learn new words.

3.4 Making Speeches and Presentations Learn how to gain confidence through preparation, and to use speaking opportunities to further your career.

3.5 Presenting Ideas and Concepts Visually Look at different kinds of visual aids, the advantages and disadvantages of each, and understand how to use images to better communicate with an audience.

Why It's Important

Top managers all agree that good communicators make good professionals. After all, business is largely a communication process. Communication is the purpose of telephones, e-mail, meetings, reports, computers, presentations, marketing, brochures, sales presentation, speeches, and even clothing and haircuts.

Don't think that communication is a specialized field that doesn't involve you. If you're in business, you're in communication. You need to know how to write well and speak before groups. You need a versatile vocabulary. You need to know the role of visual aids when you make presentations about your company, products, or projects. You also need to apply your intelligence to problem solving. These tasks can sound a bit daunting, but with a little knowledge and a lot of preparation, you can use your communication skills to prove your professionalism and advance your career!

Chapter Objectives

After completing this chapter, you will be able to:

• Write more clearly and logically in the language and formats of business.

• Solve problems by thinking critically and creatively.

• Expand your vocabulary by using a dictionary and understanding the principles behind words.

• Effectively and confidently present information to an audience.

• Use visual aids and graphic explanations to present ideas and concepts.

Set the *Pace*

Communication Communication includes every way in which information moves from one person's brain to someone else's. It includes everything from smoke signals to e-mail, from whistles to conference calls, from Morse code to computer code, from drawings in the dust to multimedia presentations on a screen.

• How many kinds of communication have you used? Try to list them all.
• What kinds of communication are most difficult for you? Which are easiest?
• What kinds of communication make you uncomfortable?

Activity In the journal section of your career portfolio, write two paragraphs: one about how much you like to use a certain kind of communication (such as e-mail, telephone, or chatting in person) and one about a certain kind of communication that bothers or scares you (such as computers or public speaking). Explain on paper why you like or dislike each. Then, share your fears and preferences with your classmates in a discussion about the powers and problems of communication.

Communicating in Writing

The written word holds a powerful place in the world of business. It is different from the spoken word—more serious, more organized, and more permanent. If any one skill is important in virtually every area of business, this is it. Professionals who master the skill of expressing themselves in writing are among the most likely to succeed. Because the written word is so important, people who can write well tend to become business leaders.

Working with Words. Good writing is not an artistic talent that one either has or doesn't have. It is something that anyone can learn. It's a matter of organizing ideas and putting some thought into the meaning and power of words. You can do it.

Reading and Study Tip

Analysis
The tips and questions throughout this section show what should and should not be found in good writing. Copy these tips and questions on a separate piece of paper in the form of a checklist. As you read through the section, check off instances where you think the writer uses each technique.

❝ *Good writing is clear thinking made visible.* **❞**

Bill Wheeler,
Technology Consultant and Writer

communication media means of relating information

The Nature of Writing

Writing and speaking both involve words, but there are some fundamental differences between these two **communication media,** that is, these two means of conveying information.

- Written words tend to be permanent.
- Written words are taken more seriously.
- Written words can be revised before anyone sees them.
- Written words are assumed to be accurate.
- Written words can be precisely duplicated.
- Written words can be reproduced and distributed.
- Written words can be organized so that it's easy for readers to find specific information.
- Written words can go where their writer can't.

Each of these special powers of the written word has advantages and disadvantages. By thinking about what you are writing, you can maximize the advantages and minimize the disadvantages.

Thinking about Your Words

When you are writing for a business purpose, you cannot simply scribble something down and be done with it. Take the time to do it correctly. The writing process involves three stages of thought: before you write, while you write, and after you've written.

Before You Write

You should think about a few things before you actually start to write. Use these questions as guidelines for prewriting:

What Do You Want to Say?   Your real message may be stated in a simple sentence, or it may require many pages of explanation. Before you start to write, think about the message that you want the reader to understand. Then you can think about how best to communicate that idea.

Should the Message Really Be in Writing?   If you want your words to be permanent or distributed to many people, it's best to present them in written form. This is also true if the information is complicated. But if just one person needs the information and it's simple to understand, a quick conversation might be the most efficient way to deliver the message. Likewise, if you don't want the information to spread, or if you're unsure of your words or what you want to say, don't put it in writing.

What's the Best Structure?   Before you write, plan a structure for your message. The structure should make it easier for the reader to understand what you are saying and to find specific information.

For example, a report on delivery problems might be structured so that it has several parts: an introduction followed by sections on (1) the types of problems, (2) the causes of the problems, (3) possible solutions to the problems, and (4) the costs of the possible solutions. Each section might have subsections with titles in bold print.

What's the Best Order of Information?   Structure also might be a matter of putting information in the right order. You might describe an incident in chronological order, starting at the beginning. You might describe a companywide situation by describing each department separately. You might organize a sales report by product, region, sales representative, or buyer. You might explain a problem by following a chain of cause-and-effect, starting at either the final effect or the initial cause.

What's the Best Medium?   Should your words be in the form of an e-mail, a letter on paper, a report, a memo, or even a handwritten note? Does your company prefer a certain format for each kind of writing? In general, you will want to use the simplest and most appropriate medium for the message.

What Information Should Be Included?   The readers of your message will assume that you have thought it out and included all relevant information. Before you start writing, you may want to list all the information you should include. At the same time, too much information can hide the important information.

As You Write

After you have planned out your writing, you can actually start to write. As you choose your words and construct your sentences, let the following rules guide you.

Be clear. Clarity takes top priority. As you write each sentence, ask yourself whether your words are easy to understand. Reading your words out loud really will help you catch confusing sentences.
Be considerate. Think about the feelings of your reader. Hurting someone's feelings with poorly chosen words will not help you communicate your message. When criticizing your reader, begin your message with some compliments. When delivering bad news, begin and end your message with something upbeat and hopeful. Remember to say *please* and *thank you.*
Be correct. There's no excuse for putting a mistake in writing. Take time to verify your facts, check your spelling, and make sure your message is perfectly clear. Before you use a word, make sure you know exactly what it

> " Say all you have to say in the fewest possible words, or your reader will be sure to skip them, and in the plainest possible words or he will certainly misunderstand them. "
>
> *John Ruskin,*
> *19th Century British Author and Art Critic*

means. Before you cite a fact, make sure it's true. Don't crust your computer spell-checker to recognize that "c-r-u-s-t" is a misspelling of "t-r-u-s-t." Before you send your message, it's a good idea to let someone else read it over to look for errors and unclear passages.

Be logical. Every sentence should connect logically to the sentence that precedes it and the one that follows it. Each paragraph should be about one topic, and usually that topic is stated in the paragraph's first sentence.

Be simple. Simple writing is good writing. Use short, simple words. Write short, simple sentences.

Let format help you. Make your page look easy to read. Use paragraph indentations, **subheads** (short titles of subsections, often in bold or italic font), and lists to leave white space among the words.

- Use **bullets** (the little dot at the beginning of this line is a bullet) to make lists easy to find and read.
- Use *italics* and **bold** fonts to make it easy to find key information.

After You Write

Professional writers know that the real writing begins after you've written the first draft. Whether you are writing a simple e-mail or a full-length report, you will always need to revise.

- Consider how you might reorganize the information.
- Look for mistakes in grammar, spelling, and facts.
- Delete unnecessary words and information.
- Consider whether your message needs more specific information or details.
- Read each sentence out loud to see if it sounds clear and logical.
- Reconsider your tone. Don't let it sound too negative or angry.
- Make sure your message relates what you really want to say.

Letters, Memos, E-Mail

Letters, memos, and e-mail are the main forms of written business communication. Few people will praise a well-written memo, but almost everyone will criticize a badly written one. Formats vary from company to company, but they tend to follow certain general guidelines.

Business Letters

The **format** of a business letter—its standard form and structure—is usually rather formal. Your company may have a preferred format, or you may want to adopt a particular format recommended by a book about business writing. Your company probably uses **letterhead,** that is, letter paper printed with the name, address, and logo of the company in a unique format and color. Before you write a letter, check with your co-workers to see how letters are formatted at your company. Also, make sure you are authorized to speak for your company.

Memorandums

Memorandums, also known as **memos,** are official written messages from one individual to another individual or group within the same company. A memo also may be sent to someone outside the company, such as a client, with whom you correspond regularly.

Tips From a Mentor

Business Letter Do's and Don'ts

- *Address a letter with a person's name.* Don't address letters impersonally. Don't use "Dear Sir," "Dear Sirs," "Dear Sir/Madam," or "To Whom It May Concern," if you can help it. (See figure 3.1)

- *Don't presume* you are writing to a man or woman. Avoid gender problems by addressing a letter to a full name, such as "Dear Pat Smith:"

- *Do use "Ms."* for a woman. It is always correct when addressing a female. Only use "Mrs." if the person has signed a letter as such.

- *Don't address someone by first name only* unless you have an established personal relationship with him or her. Even then, if your letter is formal, use the full name, and sign with your full name.

- *Do your homework* to find out a person's job title and full name. Go online to company Web sites, refer to business cards, and, if necessary, call the company receptionist and ask.

- *Do send letters to the appropriate people.* Don't send a résumé to the company CEO when there is an H.R. department. Don't send a complaint to the business manager, when it should go to the customer service department.

- *Do introduce yourself and your reason for writing* in the first paragraph. Include, if possible, a sincere greeting, like "I hope this letter finds you well and busy with new projects. I am working on a new marketing plan at the moment, and could use your advice."

- *Don't be too brief or direct* in your writing. This appears too cold or demanding. Be clear so the reader knows what you want.

- *Do include all relevant information* in a clear and logical sequence instead of presuming the reader knows or remembers what you're writing about.

- *Do politely request what you need.* Most companies will not offer anything without being asked. Be specific in describing what you need from them, whether it's a refund, some information, or a simple reply.

Memos are official documents that are often distributed widely and filed for future reference. Though they are less formal than business letters, they must avoid emotional statements and must include all of the information needed by everyone who receives it. Memos should be very clear and specific, especially when discussing a plan of action.

Your company probably has a specific format for memos. If not, make sure the format you use includes the following information:

- The date.
- Your name.
- The name of the person to whom you're sending the memo.
- The names of people receiving copies of the memo.
- A line stating the subject of the memo, often indicated by "Re:" (an abbreviation for "Regarding:").
- Your signature or written initials.

Figure 3.1 *Sample Letters*

20650 North 58th Avenue, Apt. 15A
Glendale, AZ 85308
August 17, 2002

Ms. Jaclyn Abel
~~Director of Public Relations~~ *No title*
~~Heard Museum~~
2301 North Central Avenue
Phoenix, AZ 85004

        Jaclyn, ⟵——— *Informal greeting*
Dear ~~Ms. Abel:~~

I am writing to apply for the position of Public Relations Assistant
that you recently advertised in the *Arizona Republic*. ~~I believe that
my experience and qualifications fit well with your needs at the
Heard, a museum that I have visited and loved all my life.~~
                Does not show confidence in experience
No mention of resume
~~As the enclosed résumé indicates,~~ I have experience in the public
relations field. While at Arizona State University West, I worked
as an intern in the Public Relations Office~~, where I was responsible
for analyzing and reporting on the image projected by the university's
external publications~~. I also had a hand in creating the brochure
for the University College Center and participated in planning ASU
West's "Dream Big" campaign. ~~I also assisted in organizing an
opening convocation attended by 800 people. This work in the not-
for-profit sector has prepared me well for employment at the Heard.~~
    Does not explain how school experience applies to the job
Additionally, my undergraduate major in American History has helped
me understand the rich heritage of Native Americans. ~~In my senior
thesis, which received the Westmarc Writing Award, I studied the
history of the relationship between the Hopis and the Anglo population
as reflected in photographs taken from 1920 to 1940. Although my
thesis focuses on a specific tribe,~~ I have been interested for many
years in Native-American culture and have often made use of resources
in the Heard. ~~I think that I would do a superior job of presenting
the Heard as the premier museum of Native American culture.~~

Confidential reference letters are available from ASU West Career
Services. I sincerely hope that we will have an opportunity to talk
further about the Heard Museum and its outstanding cultural
contributions to the Phoenix metropolitan area.
~~Please contact me at 623-555-7310.~~ *No contact information*

Sincerely,

Laura Amabisca

~~Laura Amabisca~~ *Does not make name easy to read*

~~Enc.~~

Thinking Critically Present your professional attitude by following the correct format of a business letter. *Which letter-writer would you be most likely to help?*

E-Mail

E-mail is a relatively new means of communication, so it does not yet have any formal formats such as those used in business letters. In general, you can't go wrong by following the format and language style of a memo or a business letter. Do not use the uncon-

20650 North 58th Avenue, Apt. 15A
Glendale, AZ 85308
August 17, 2002

Ms. Jaclyn Abel
Director of Public Relations
Heard Museum
2301 North Central Avenue
Phoenix, AZ 85004

Dear Ms. Abel:

I am writing to apply for the position of Public Relations Assistant
that you recently advertised in the *Arizona Republic*. I believe that
my experience and qualifications fit well with your needs at the
Heard, a museum that I have visited and loved all my life.

As the enclosed résumé indicates, I have experience in the public
relations field. While at Arizona State University West, I worked
as an intern in the Public Relations Office, where I was responsible
for analyzing and reporting on the image projected by the university's
external publications. I also had a hand in creating the brochure
for the University College Center and participated in planning ASU
West's "Dream Big" campaign. I also assisted in organizing an
opening convocation attended by 800 people. This work in the not-
for-profit sector has prepared me well for employment at the Heard.

Additionally, my undergraduate major in American History has helped
me understand the rich heritage of Native Americans. In my senior
thesis, which received the Westmarc Writing Award, I studied the
history of the relationship between the Hopis and the Anglo population
as reflected in photographs taken from 1920 to 1940. Although my
thesis focuses on a specific tribe, I have been interested for many
years in Native-American culture and have often made use of resources
in the Heard. I think that I would do a superior job of presenting
the Heard as the premier museum of Native-American culture.

Confidential reference letters are available from ASU West Career
Services. I sincerely hope that we will have an opportunity to talk
further about the Heard Museum and its outstanding cultural
contributions to the Phoenix metropolitan area.
Please contact me at 623-555-7310.

Sincerely,

Laura Amabisca

Laura Amabisca

Enc.

---

ventional grammar and spelling seen in some Internet chat rooms. As in a memo, e-mail
should be clear and specific and include all relevant information. Using the "reply" feature of e-mail applications will help your reader remember what you're discussing.

As you know, e-mail can easily be forwarded to people you never intended to
receive it. Be careful what you say. Avoid too much informality. Learn about proper
netiquette, or good manners for cyberspace (see Business Skills Brush-Up for
Chapter One). Let every e-mail reflect your professionalism.

netiquette good manners for communicating by e-mail

Reports

There are many kinds of reports: sales reports, progress reports, problem reports, meeting reports, and many more. If you're expected to write a report, your company probably has examples of similar reports. You can use these old reports to learn the preferred format. When you study them, look for these characteristics:

- How is the report divided? Into sections? By product? By department? By time period?
- How are titles and subheads used to categorize information into sections?
- What kind of data, such as financial figures, production levels, and so forth, is provided?
- Is there a number system for organizing sections?

QUICK RECAP 3.1

COMMUNICATING IN WRITING

- Writing is different from speaking because it's permanent, easily distributed, and assumed to be complete and accurate.
- Before you write, think about what you want to say, decide whether writing is the best way to say it, consider how to structure the message, and make sure you know what information to include.
- As you write, monitor your words for clarity. Write correct sentences in a logical sequence and in a tone that does not offend others or cause unnecessary conflict.
- After you write, always revise.
- Business letters must avoid threatening or offensive language.
- Memos are written to people in your company or to people close to your company, such as regular clients.
- E-mail should avoid the unconventional grammar and spelling found in chat rooms.
- Reports usually follow a format designed by your company.

CHECK YOURSELF

1. How are written messages different from spoken messages?
2. What elements of good writing should you keep in mind as you write?

Check your answers online at **www.mhhe.com/pace.**

BUSINESS VOCABULARY

bullet   a dot marking an item in a list
communication media   means of relating information
format   the standard form and structure of formal written communication
letterhead   letter paper printed with the name, address, and logo of the company in a unique format and color
memorandum (or memo)   official written message from one individual to another individual or to a group, usually within the same company
netiquette   good manners for communicating by e-mail
subheads   short subject titles

Thinking Critically and Creatively

One ability is expected of all professionals: the ability to *think and make good decisions.* Once you rise above the lowest rungs of the career ladder, you may find yourself in situations where a solution or a decision is not immediately apparent. You will have to apply some thought to the situation and decide how to handle it. This, essentially, is the job of every professional.

Think Critically; Think Creatively.   Your skills, experience, and education are the tools you bring to your trade, but it is your brain that will tell you what to do with these tools. It's important that you know how to think *critically* and *creatively* so that you can grapple with the situations that you, as a professional, are expected to resolve.

Problems in the World of Business

Problems are a natural part of business. Some problems are a matter of things not working as they should: sales decline, shipments get lost, workers go on strike, new regulations require change, products are returned with defects. Other problems are a matter of improvement: increasing sales, decreasing costs, facing new competition, building a better product, training new employees. Some problems just look like decisions that have to be made.

As a professional, you will be expected to identify problems, find solutions, and make good decisions. Good professionals are good problem solvers, and those who can solve problems are those who will rise to the upper levels of management.

Two Ways to Solve Problems

Critical thinking and creative thinking are two basic approaches to problem solving. Both are effective, but each works better when it works hand-in-hand with the other.

Critical Thinking

Critical thinking is a logical, analytical, methodical approach to understanding a problem and working toward a solution. Scientists and mathematicians tend to use critical thinking to solve problems.

Creative Thinking

Creative thinking is an intuitive, nonlogical approach to solving a problem by being open to inspiration from unexpected sources. Writers, artists, and inventors tend to use creative thinking to find solutions, sometimes even before they identify the problem!

Reading and Study Tip

Drawing Conclusions
Isolating a question to answer or a point you want to make is an important part of critical thinking. Analyze information, ideas, and arguments to come up with conclusions about your point or question. Think of a question for this section such as, *Which is more effective— critical or creative thinking?* On a separate sheet of paper, write your conclusions.

---

critical thinking a logical, analytical, methodical approach to understanding a problem and working toward a solution

creative thinking an intuitive, nonlogical approach to solving a problem by being open to inspiration from unexpected sources

---

Critical Thinking

Critical thinking involves focusing on a problem, understanding its parts, gathering and assessing information, and considering possible solutions. It's a very logical, step-by-step process.

" Think as you work, for in the final analysis, your worth to your company comes not only in solving problems, but also in anticipating them. "

Harold Wallace Ross,
Editor and Founder of
The New Yorker

1. **Start with a positive attitude.** Approach the problem as a challenge that you know you can solve. You *want* to question it, study it, understand it, and solve it. Remember that working hard to deal with this problem will make you a stronger professional.

2. **Define the problem.** Define the problem by examining it closely. Can you find the cause of the problem? Does the problem have parts that can be solved separately? Is the problem part of a bigger picture that involves other problems? Are you accepting someone else's definition of the problem without questioning it?

3. **Gather necessary information.** You will need information about the problem and its possible solutions. You must think about what kinds of information you need. What questions should you be asking? What solutions have worked or failed in the past, and why? Is this problem like any other problems your company has had? Is there a pattern to the problem? Is it a problem with people, things, or systems? What kinds of data are available? Who can help you find information? What theories, principles, formulas, rules, calculations, research, and so on, might apply to the problem?

4. **Apply creative thinking.** As explained below, you can use creative thinking to look for entirely new ideas that might solve the problem.

5. **Avoid common obstacles.**
   - Don't assume that old solutions and expert advice are necessarily correct.
   - Don't see people as **stereotypes,** that is, as having all the characteristics you expect in people like them.
   - Don't make snap decisions. Get all relevant information before deciding.
   - Don't generalize about people, problems, or solutions. No two people are the same. A problem may not be the same as a similar problem. Solutions for similar problems may not work.
   - Don't give up because the problem seems too hard to solve.
   - Don't ignore the problem.

6. **Develop a hypothesis.** A **hypothesis** is a possible but unproven solution. If possible, develop and assess other hypotheses. Then you can try the one that seems most likely to work first.

7. **Test your hypothesis.** If it isn't too expensive, time-consuming, dangerous, or otherwise difficult, try your hypothesis to see if it works. If you can't try it on an experimental basis, use all available information to predict whether it is likely to work. If you have more than one hypothesis, start with the one that seems most likely to work. Before you try a second hypothesis, analyze why the first one failed.

8. **Be persistent.** Don't let a problem get the better of you. Keep thinking about it. Gather more information. Ask for help. Look for completely different solutions. Put the problem in the back of your mind and think about something else for a while.

stereotype a mistaken impression that a person shares all the characteristics of similar people

hypothesis a possible but unproven solution

" Let your thoughts meander towards a sea of ideas. "

Leo D. Minnigh,
Author

Creative Thinking

Creative thinking doesn't focus on the problem as much as critical thinking does, and it doesn't aim so directly at the solution. It doesn't depend so much on infor-

Problem Solving

Your Challenge

You work as an analyst in a marketing and sales department. You have been sitting at your desk all day trying to work out a solution to a problem. Your division didn't meet its sales numbers for the quarter and you are trying to figure out why. You have been poring over your sales reports and just can't seem to narrow the problem down. There is just so much information and so many factors to consider, how do you locate the source of the problem, let alone solve it?! You are getting very stressed out and you feel like your brain is fried. What do you do?

The Possibilities

A. Tell your boss you have looked through all the information and there just doesn't seem to be an explanation for the problem. Blame it on a poor economy or the sales reps having a bad month and leave it to address next month.

B. Organize the information you are working with into a database with sales territories, companies, customer profiles, and ordering history. Look for patterns of behavior and ask critical questions like *Have sales dropped in one geographic territory, among one specific group?*

C. Make a checklist of all the factors that you know could affect sales, anything from your best salesperson being away on vacation to increased competition. Go to lunch and let these questions work in your subconscious mind. Come back with a clear mind and then check the facts to see if you are on the right track.

D. Keep looking at the numbers and figures until you can't focus anymore. Tell yourself you have to figure this out and you can't do anything else until you get it. Put the pressure on yourself so you will be forced to come up with an answer.

Your Solution

Choose the solution that you think will be most effective and write a few sentences explaining your opinion. Then check your answer with the answer on our Web site: **www.mhhe.com/pace.**

mation and logic. It tends to wander toward a solution, looking into possibilities that the critical thinker might never think of using.

1. **Start with a positive attitude.** Tell yourself that somewhere there is a solution no one has ever thought of before. Logic won't take you to that place, but "free thinking" might. You might find the answer by *not* looking for it.

2. **Look at the problem in a different way.** Compare the problem to something else. Look at declining sales, for example, as an ax that needs sharpening or as a car with an engine problem. Imagine the problem the way someone else (a child, a foreigner, a squirrel, a soldier, a shoe) might see it. Consider whether the problem might actually be an opportunity.

3. **Seek other routes to a solution.** Rather than following a logical path toward a solution, take other paths and look in other places. Can you compare the problem to something in nature and consider nature's solution? Can you convert the problem to a game or puzzle and think of it that way? Can you and some of your more creative friends **brainstorm**—a group process of tossing out crazy ideas and looking for ways that one of them might actually work? Try writing a poem about the problem or drawing a picture of it. Challenge the rules or traditions that seem to prevent a solution. Put the problem in the back of your mind, change your daily routine as much as possible, and be alert for hints at solutions in unexpected events.

Dr. Joe Pace
IMAGINATION

"A mind once stretched by a new idea never regains its original dimensions."

brainstorm a group process of tossing out ideas and looking for ways that one of them might actually work

Figure 3.2 *Two Processes*

Brainard's Critical Thinking Process	Sonia's Creative Thinking Process
He approaches the problem as a challenge he can conquer.	She's sure she'll find inspiration if she keeps looking for it.
He defines the problem very carefully and logically.	She defines the problem very loosely, as having something to do with snacks.
He gathers all the facts so he can think about them.	She looks for answers by comparing other things to the problem.
The facts and his analysis lead logically to a workable solution—his hypothesis.	She makes a connection—a hypothesis—between two things that have little to do with each other.
He develops a plan for testing his hypothesis.	She develops a plan for testing her hypothesis.

Thinking Critically Both processes to problem solving worked. Brainard and Sonia got to the same idea by following different paths. *Which way do you problem-solve best?*

4. **Apply critical thinking.** Creative thinking alone probably won't generate a solution, but if you can shift between critical (logical, methodical) thinking and creative thinking, your mind may open on new horizons. After creative thinking leads to inspiration, shift to critical thinking to make the idea a reality.
5. **Avoid obstacles to creativity.**
   • Don't judge ideas until you've considered every way they might work.
   • Don't presume that experts and authorities are right.
   • Don't ignore your intuition.
   • Don't be afraid of failure.
   • Don't criticize other people's ideas while paying no attention to their criticism of your ideas.
   • Don't think you can't be creative.
   • Don't look for reasons why ideas won't work. Look for ways to make them work.
6. **Develop a hypothesis—even a crazy one.** If a vague solution somehow feels right, work with it. Don't wait for a perfect solution to present itself.
7. **Test your hypothesis.** If it isn't too hard to test your idea, go ahead and try it even if you don't think it will work. The results might inspire a better solution. Or maybe you can test it in some creative way, using other materials or situations. The testing itself might inspire new ideas.
8. **Be persistent.** Keep thinking about it. Keep *not* thinking about it. Roll it around your conscious mind, then store it in the back of your mind for a while, then think about it again. Think of more creative techniques for seeking a solution. Keep asking other people. Sleep on it.

Don't Give Up!

It is easy to become frustrated and want to give up when trying to solve a difficult problem. Now you have two new methods of problem solving to try. Start with the one you feel most comfortable with. If you still haven't found an answer, try the other method. Continue to develop both your critical thinking and your creative thinking skills!

QUICK RECAP 3.2

THINKING CRITICALLY AND CREATIVELY

- Critical thinking is a logical, analytical, methodical approach to understanding a problem and working toward a solution.
- Creative thinking is an intuitive, nonlogical approach to solving a problem by being open to inspiration from unexpected sources.
- Critical thinking begins with a definition of the problem and the gathering of all related information.
- To think creatively, look at the problem in different ways, comparing it to other problems.
- Use information to develop a hypothesis, then test it.

CHECK YOURSELF

1. What is the difference between critical thinking and creative thinking?
2. How can creative thinking be part of critical thinking, and critical thinking be part of creative thinking?

Check your answers online at **www.mhhe.com/pace.** *Pace* ONLINE

BUSINESS VOCABULARY

brainstorm   a group process of tossing out ideas and looking for ways that one of them might actually work

creative thinking   an intuitive, nonlogical approach to solving a problem by being open to inspiration from unexpected sources

critical thinking   a logical, analytical, methodical approach to understanding a problem and working toward a solution

hypothesis   a possible but unproven solution

stereotype   a mistaken impression that a person shares all the characteristics of similar people

Developing Your Vocabulary

As you learned in the first section of this chapter, words are powerful tools. Using the right words at the right time makes that tool even more powerful. English is an especially rich language because it pulls words from many different ancient languages, from Greek to Latin to German to Hebrew. A good dictionary may have over 200,000 words listed. If you can master the wealth of the English language, you can be more persuasive, more informative, and more professional.

Watch your Words. You don't need to memorize a dictionary to develop a powerful vocabulary. If you learn a few of the principles of vocabulary, get in the habit of using a dictionary, and acknowledge the importance of continually expanding your vocabulary, you will soon find yourself wielding words with power and confidence.

❝ *For good or ill, your conversation is your advertisement. Every time you open your mouth, you let men look into your mind. Do they see it well clothed, neat, business-wise?* ❞

Bruce Burton,
Author

Reading and Study Tip

Dictionary Skills
When reading this section, keep a dictionary handy. Pick five words in the text that aren't defined and look them up in a dictionary, even if you think you know what they mean. On a separate sheet of paper, write whether or not you knew the correct meaning for the word and how many different meanings there are for the word; write sentences that use each meaning of the word.

jargon words that are used in specific fields and trades

technical words words that are used in specific fields and trades that are strictly technical in nature, especially scientific words

vogue words words that come into style, often replacing other perfectly correct words

euphemisms relatively soft words that replace harsher words

acronyms words formed by the first letters in a phrase, such as ROM in CD-ROM

You and Your Words

The words you choose to use in writing and conversation determine to a great extent what people think of you and how they accept your ideas. Ideas expressed in the right words are more likely to be respected and accepted. Knowing which words to use is dependent on having the right words at your disposal when you need them.

Types of Business Words

Listening to a conversation about a different industry can be like trying to understand a foreign language. Even most hobbies have their own vocabulary. Companies often use familiar words in unconventional ways. Business vocabulary tends to include various types of words:

- **Jargon** consists of words that are used in specific fields and trades. Medicine, law, mining, information technology, publishing—each of these has its own vocabulary.
- **Technical words** are similar to jargon but are strictly technical in nature, especially scientific words such as those relating to chemistry, geology, botany, and so forth.
- **Vogue words** are words that come into style and become a kind of business slang, often replacing other perfectly correct words. For example, "bottom line" replaces "result" and "address an issue" replaces "discuss a problem."
- **Euphemisms** are relatively soft words that replace harsher words, such as "downsizing" for "firing" and "senior citizen" for "old person."
- **Acronyms** are words formed by the first letters of a phrase. A well-known acronym is *radar,* which is short for *ra*dio *d*etecting *a*nd *r*anging.

Other Kinds of Words

Normal conversation tends to use a couple of other kinds of words:

- **Slang** is informal language that is considered correct but acceptable only in informal situations. Slang is useful for presenting ideas in a down-to-earth way. Examples of slang include *rip off* (meaning *steal*), *head honcho* (meaning *boss*), *dough* (meaning *money*), and *in the ballpark* (meaning *approximately*).
- *Nonwords and meaningless words* are expressions such as *ummm . . .*, *hey, you know,* and the odd use of *like* to depict situations, as in "she was, like, so disappointed." These are not expressions to put in writing, and it's best to minimize or avoid them in professional conversations.
- **Vulgarity** includes offensive and dirty words, the swears, the curses—you know the ones. Vulgarity also includes the offensive words sometimes used for people of certain nationalities, religions, and other groupings. You can't go wrong by simply not using vulgarity. If you tend to use vulgar words, you'd best get out of the habit.

slang informal language that is considered correct but acceptable only in informal situations

vulgarity offensive and "dirty" words, including the offensive words sometimes used for people of certain nationalities, religions, races, and other groupings

Learning New Words

You can't learn a vast new vocabulary all at once. But you can learn new words little by little, gradually building up an impressive vocabulary that will help you communicate more effectively. Expanding your vocabulary is mostly a matter of attitude. If you recognize the power and importance of words, you'll soon find yourself packing a powerful vocabulary. It does, however, take a little effort. Here are some vocabulary-building strategies:

- *Use a dictionary.* If you don't know the precise meaning of a word, look it up. Jot down the basic meaning so you can review it later. If you use a computer, a software dictionary would be a good investment. (See below for tips on making the best use of a dictionary.)
- *Look for new words.* You'll find the jargon and technical terms of your business in **trade publications,** the magazines and newspapers that deal exclusively with a given business or industry. Watch for those words. If you can't find them in a dictionary, ask someone. When you hear someone speaking intelligently, listen to the words they use.
- *Practice new words.* When you learn a new word, write it and speak it in a sentence or two. This will help you remember it and use it more easily when an opportunity arises. Try to use the word in conversation.
- *Study speeches.* Trade conferences and seminars often feature speakers who discuss current topics in their field. They use the current vocabulary. Listen to these speeches not only for information but also for the words used. Sometimes you can find transcripts of these speeches on the Internet; you also can request them from the speaker's organization.
- *Read.* Beyond any doubt, reading is the best way to absorb new words and learn correct grammer. As you read, analyze words and sentences to make sure you understand how they are used and constructed.
- *Observe your own words.* Listen to the way you speak. Do you use complete sentences? Do you stud your sentences with meaningless words such as *um, yeah, like,* and *ya' know?* Strive to sound like your boss's boss, not a high school student.
- *Learn the roots of words.* Many words are built of parts that relate to other words. For example, *pre-* refers to something that happened before something else, as in *pre-Reagan. Socio-* refers to society, so *socio economics* would refer to the social aspect of economics.
- *Study "trouble words."* If you have trouble with certain words, such as the difference between *lie* and *lay,* the exact meaning of *chagrin,* or the correct American spelling of *judgment* (no *e* in the middle), look them up and jot down what you need to remember. Do this *before* the word comes up in conversation or writing.

> *One forgets words as one forgets names. One's vocabulary needs constant fertilizing or it will die.*
>
> *Evelyn Waugh,*
> *British Satirical Novelist*

trade publications magazines and newspapers that deal exclusively with a given business or industry

---

Internet Quest

Word of the Day

Search for "word of the day" services and sign up to have a new vocabulary word e-mailed to you each day. Learning a new word every day will help you build your vocabulary.

Pace Points

Show Off

Never use words whose meaning you don't know. You may hear popular phrases and expressions in the workplace or hear your boss using big impressive-sounding words. Only use these words after you have looked them up and are sure of what they mean and imply. Nothing looks worse than showing off with a big word, especially if you use it in correctly.

Use a Dictionary

Get used to using a dictionary. It may be more useful than you think. It can give you not only the spelling and meaning of a word but also the history of the word, the meaning of its parts, other words that mean almost the same thing, and the proper use of the word. Here are some things to note when you look up a word:

1. *The spelling.* Check the spelling of not only the word itself (*lie*, for example) but, if it's a verb, the past tense (*lay*) and the past participle (*lain*, as in *I have lain*). Note the spelling of the -ing form (*lying*). If it's a noun (*roof*, for example), note the plural (*roofs*, not *rooves*).

2. *The parts of the word.* A good dictionary will break the word into parts. As you look at each part, think of other words that have similar parts and perhaps similar meanings. For example, *autobiography* consists of *auto-*, meaning *self*; *bio*, referring to *life*; and *–graph-*, referring to something written or studied. You can probably think of other words that include *auto-*, such as *automatic* and *automation*. *Bio-* may remind you of words relating to life, such as *biology* and *biopsy*. *-graphy* may remind you of other words dealing with writing or the study of something, such as *geography* and *autograph*. Looking up *geography*, you will learn that *geo-* refers to the earth, making it easier for you to guess the meaning of *geohabitat* or even a technical word that's not in the dictionary, such as *geophotography*. The more you study these parts of words, the easier it will be to learn new words.

3. *Related phrases.* A good dictionary will note phrases that include the word you looked up. For example, the definition of *follow* may include definitions of *follow up, follow through, follow along, follow suit, follow your nose*, and so on. If English is not your native language, be sure you get a dictionary that lists these phrases and expressions.

Online dictionaries can be very user-friendly, especially if you are not sure how to spell a word. When you type in a word, it will give many variations, making it easier to find the word you want. some online dictionaries also use sound files so you can hear how to pronounce the word.

QUICK RECAP 3.3

DEVELOPING YOUR VOCABULARY

- Words are powerful tool in business, especially when you have the right word available at the right time.
- Business language employs jargon, technical words, vogue words, euphemisms, and even slang, but vulgarity and meaningless nonwords are to be avoided.
- To expand your vocabulary, use a dictionary, look for new words in trade publications, read a lot, and listen for new words in conversation and speeches.
- When you look upon a word, check not only its spelling and meaning but also its parts and related phrases.

CHECK YOURSELF

1. What kinds of words should a good professional try to avoid?
2. List ways to learn new vocabulary words.

BUSINESS VOCABULARY

acronyms   words formed by the first letters in a phrase, such as ROM in CD-ROM

euphemisms   relatively soft words that replace harsher words

jargon   words that are used in specify fields and trades

slang   informal language that is considered correct but acceptable only in informal situations

technical words   words that are used in specific fields and trades that are strictly technical in nature, especially scientific words

trade publications   magazines and newspapers that deal exclusively with a given business or industry

vogue words   words that come into style, often replacing other perfectly correct words.

vulgarity   offensive and "dirty" words, including the offensive words sometimes used for people of certain nationalities, religions, races, and other groupings

Making Speeches and Presentations

Many people are struck cold with terror at the thought of giving a speech or presentation before a group of people. Certainly, delivering information to a group is a challenging situation that leaves the speaker open to embarrassment. But standing up in front of a lot of people doesn't have to be traumatic. Rather, public speaking and presentations should be an opportunity to demonstrate that you are knowledgeable and have prepared yourself to instruct others.

Stand Up; Speak Up. The trick to successful presentations is to build up your confidence with excellent preparation. Professionals are asked to make a presentation only when they know something that other people don't. You're working hard to become that kind of professional, so you'd be wise to learn how to make a professional presentation.

Reading and Study Tip

Reading Aloud
Read this section aloud while paying attention to how you pronounce words and how punctuation affects the rhythm and flow of the sentence. Then pick one paragraph. Find the main ideas in each sentence. Read the paragraph out loud to a friend or classmate, presenting the information and stressing the important ideas as you read. Ask them if they could tell what ideas you were trying to stress.

> It takes one hour of preparation for each minute of presentation time.
>
> *Wayne Burgraff,*
> Author

visual aids Charts, graphs, and other images that let audience members use their eyes to process a message

You're the Expert

If you're asked to speak before a group, it's because you know something that other people want to learn. *You're* the expert. When you have an opportunity to give a speech or presentation, it's an opportunity to demonstrate your competence and professionalism. It's also an opportunity to further your career.

Even before you start, the audience believes you are an expert in the topic you're going to present. The advantage is yours as long as you are prepared.

Prepare, Prepare, Prepare

You'll probably have plenty of time to prepare. Don't wait until the last minute, and don't count on being able to bluff your way through without preparation. *You will find confidence through preparation.* Your preparation should involve five steps.

1. *Know your audience.* The person who called upon you to speak should be able to tell you about the kinds of people you'll find in the audience. Are they professionals in a given field? Potential customers? People already in favor of or against what you are going to talk about? People who already know a lot or a little or nothing about your topic? Think about what these people want to know, then think about what you need to do to get your message across.

2. *Gather your tools.* What will help you get your message across? **Visual aids** are images and objects that let your audience use their eyes as well as their ears to take in your message. Visual aids can include a blackboard, a flip chart, a slide projector, a PowerPoint program, or a video program. You may want to hand out brochures, product specifications, data displayed in graphics or spreadsheets, or other kinds of written information. You may want to have samples to show or other objects for the audience to look at. *Visual displays will*

help you convey your message and keep your audience's attention. The next section of this chapter has more information about using visual aids.

3. *Gather your data.* You will probably need to present not only an idea but also the facts and data that prove your point. If you're already an expert, you already have your facts but will want to organize them. If you need to do research, use the Internet, print publications, and the advice of other experts.

4. *Write your speech.* You aren't going to *read* your speech, but you really should *write* it. It doesn't have to be the Gettysburg Address. It has to be a clear message delivered in a logical order with credible evidence to back it up.

5. *Rehearse.* Practice each sentence so you can deliver it in the right tone of voice. You want to be able to deliver your speech without reading each sentence. Try to work from an outline of your written speech.

How to Write a Good Speech

Good speeches tend to go through five stages.

1. *A joke.* Unless your speech is about a dead-serious subject, a joke is a good way to get the audience to accept you and look forward to an interesting speech. You can find books of jokes in a library or bookstore, and there are many Internet sites with jokes. You want to look for a joke that somehow relates to your topic. It doesn't have to relate very closely. In fact, a very loose connection to your topic becomes a joke in itself. You will probably have to take an existing joke and change a few details to relate it to your topic.

2. *Tell them what you're going to tell them.* In just a few sentences, outline your major points. ("Today we're going to look at three ways to improve performance . . .")

3. *Tell them.* Deliver your main points one at a time, backing each up with facts. Make it clear that you are talking about one of your main points. Say, for example, "Next I'd like to tell you about the history of this company."

4. *Tell them what you told them.* As you wrap up your speech, review your main points in a few sentences. ("So, in conclusion, as we've seen . . .")

5. *Tell them what to do.* If you expect action from you audience, such as placing an order, requesting more information, or participating in an event, tell them specifically what they should do and how they should do it. ("I'd like all of you to write down this Web site address . . .")

Tips for a Better Speech

- The shorter the better. After 20 minutes, *no one* will be listening to you.
- No one pays attention to anything for more than eight minutes, so you have to keep reminding people of what you just said.
- Jokes during the speech will do much to hold your audiences attention.
- Don't let people read while you're talking.
- If possible, involve your audience by asking relevant questions:
  - "How many here have used a digital camera?"
  - "When I say *comfortable,* what does that make you think of?"
  - "What are some of the things that concern you about having a nuclear power plant in your town?"
- Don't expect people to tell you when they don't understand.

> ❝ *No one ever complains about a speech being too short!* ❞
>
> *Ira Hayes,*
> *Native American World War II*
> *Veteran and Hero*

Pace Points

Nobody Knows

If you make a little mistake during a presentation, chances are nobody will notice. Just keep going and correct it when you have a chance. If it's a big mistake, apologize, make a joke, and move on. The point is not to interrupt your train of thought. A fuss made over a mistake is more distracting than the mistake itself.

Pace Points

Speech Warm-Ups

We all know how a powerful, clear voice can get our attention. You can use your voice as a tool to get your audience's attention. Speak clearly and loudly without shouting. Before a presentation, hum a few bars of a tune or do some tongue twisters to warm up your voice. Breathe deeply before you speak to support the sound of your voice with plenty of air. Keep your tone light and upbeat.

Good Feedback

Your Challenge

Your boss has spent a great deal of time writing a presentation she plans on giving to the board of directors to get approval for a major new project. She gives it to you and asks for your opinion. After about the fifth page, you are ready to fall asleep. The speech is long, full of too much information, and very, very boring. You don't want the board to tune out while she pitches the idea. You want to tell her what the problem is, but how?

The Possibilities

A. Go through the speech and look for blocks of information that can be represented visually. Create some sample charts and slides with bulleted lists. Take your changes to your boss and present them to her as if she were an audience member at her meeting to show how visuals will "contribute" to her speech.

B. Tell her that her speech is boring, that you almost fell asleep reading it, and that you think it needs some major work.

C. Completely rewrite the speech, in your tone of voice, adding some jokes you think she'll like and some new information, then hand it back new and improved.

D. Tell her it's great, and make sure you take a long lunch while the meeting is happening so you don't have to watch her struggle to keep the audience's attention.

Your Solution

Choose the solution that you think will be most effective and write a few sentences explaining your opinion. Then check your answer with the answer on our Web site: **www.mhhe.com/pace.**

Making Your Presentation

> *They expect a professional presentation, so they expect to see a 'professional.' Dress appropriately for the occasion, but don't be one of the crowd.*
>
> **Wess Roberts,**
> *Author on Business and Leadership Topics*

Ask yourself this: Why are you making a presentation or delivering a speech instead of just writing a report? There may be several reasons:

- You can use your voice and body language to be more communicative and persuasive.
- People would rather hear about your topic than read about it.
- Your speech may back up a report.
- You may want to answer questions from the audience.
- A presentation allows you to use sound, graphics, words, tone of voice, and audience participation to communicate your message.

Stage Fright

Stage fright is the main reason people avoid giving speeches and presentations, but usually it's *fear of* stage fright. There's nothing to fear. No one throws rotten eggs at speakers anymore. No one faints on stage. The audience will sympathize with a little nervousness. So don't worry about it.

Tips From a Mentor

Ten Tips to Better Presentations

- *Dress and groom well.* People will judge your message by your appearance. Dress just one level better than your audience. For example, if your audience will be in jeans and t-shirts, you don't need to wear a suit—wear khakis and a button-down shirt.

- *Meet with the event organizer.* If someone is in charge of the event where you will speak, talk with that person about how you'd like to be introduced and what the audience wants to hear.

- *Be silent for a moment.* When you approach the podium, be silent as you organize papers or drink a bit of water. Don't rush. Take a deep breath and relax your body as you exhale slowly. Let the audience observe you for a moment. Stand there until the audience is silent and waiting.

- *If necessary, introduce yourself.* You can skip this if someone has introduced you. If not, introduce yourself and briefly state your qualifications—but not to the point of showing off.

- *Talk slowly.* People need to think about what you're telling them. Pause often.

- *Use your body and your voice.* Let your hands express emotion. Use your fingers to indicate that you are on the first, second, or third point. If the microphone allows, move around the stage. Don't drone. When you write your speech, plan the places where you will speak more loudly or raise your pitch.

- *Maintain eye contact.* As you speak, look directly into the eyes of various people in the audience. Looking just above the last row also gives the impression that you are directly addressing your audience.

- *Don't say "OK? You know?" as you explain something.* These words can be meaningless, just as the nonwords *umm* and *uh*. Avoid any other "filler" phrases.

- *Foresee questions.* If you're going to have a question-and-answer period at the end (check with the organizer first), know what to expect. Have your answers ready, especially answers to the tough questions.

- *Don't read your speech.* Use an outline that lists your main points, but keep your head up as you speak to the audience.

- Remember: you never look as nervous as you think you look.
- If your mind goes blank—admit it. Laugh at it. This will actually endear you to your audience. Be sure you have your notes handy though, to get back on track.
- If you get lost, admit it, take a deep breath, and go through your notes. Take your time.
- Achieve confidence through preparation.
- It's okay to not know the answer to a question. Tell the person to meet you later so you can get in touch when you know the answer. People will sense if you are just making something up.

“ *The right word may be effective, but no word was ever as effective as a rightly timed pause.* ”

Mark Twain (pen name for Samuel Clemens),
Famed American Writer and Icon

New Attitudes / New Opportunities

We'd like you to meet Amy Philips, an employment lawyer in Cleveland, Ohio. We asked her about her experiences speaking in public as a litigator (handling lawsuits). Here's what she had to say about. . .

What She Does to Prepare to Make a Presentation "Probably 75 percent of the work that I do involves verbal communication. Maybe 25 percent of that 75 percent involves convincing people or a jury of an argument. So the first thing I need to know is my audience. Then, I prepare myself by knowing the facts."

Having and Building Confidence as a Speaker "The first time I gave an opening statement, I was very nervous and I spoke very quickly. Although in my head it sounded much slower than I usually speak, at the end of my opening statement, the court reporter asked to borrow my notes because she'd missed a couple of things I said because I was speaking so quickly. Ever since then, in any type of presentation, I rehearse everything I say. I try to rehearse it extra slowly. Extra slowly in my head is probably normal speech. I think that practice is what it takes."

The Importance of Appearing Confident Even if you are Nervous "The confidence comes from, again, the practice. Once you're comfortable with yourself and your speech, you'll be more confident in what you're saying and not wonder *Is my skirt straight?* or things like that. You've got to be comfortable wearing your clothes, you've got to be comfortable with your speaking voice, and you need to know your material. As long as you're prepared, you can overcome confidence problems."

How You Can Prepare for a Business Presentation "If you are going to have exhibits, charts, outlines, or preprinted materials to refer to or to hand out, make sure you know the material in them. Also, practice in front of a mirror, no matter what kind of a speech you're giving. Really, it does help. Use a tape recorder and listen to yourself. You may realize, 'Gosh, I do talk fast,' or 'I really need to learn to pronounce that word without stammering over it.' Get feedback from others—a study group or even your family."

> **❝** *Confidence and courage come through preparation and practice.* **❞**
>
> *Anonymous*

Getting Help

There are many sources that can help you gain confidence and learn to speak in public:

- Courses at community colleges and adult education.
- Books.
- Videotapes and DVDs.
- Web sites.

Two organizations help people become better public speakers:

- *Toastmasters International.* Local chapters of this dues-paying group meet regularly to practice speaking and help each other with difficulties.
- *Dale Carnegie Institute.* For a tuition fee, this organization can provide you with a series of lessons given by an authorized instructor.

QUICK RECAP 3.4

MAKING SPEECHES AND PRESENTATIONS

- An opportunity to speak is an opportunity to prove your expertise and further your career.
- Preparation is the key to a good presentation and to the confidence you need.
- To prepare, know your audience, create visual aids, know your facts, write your speech, and practice it.
- Because people have difficulty paying attention, you should tell them what you're going to tell them, then tell them, then tell them what you told them.
- Keep your speech short, and try to involve the audience.
- Dress well, talk slowly, use your body and voice to enhance your words, speak from an outline, and prepare answers to possible questions.
- Let preparation lessen stage fright.

CHECK YOURSELF

1. What should you do to prepare for a presentation or speech?
2. List what you should include in a good speech or presentation.

Check your answers online at www.mhhe.com/pace. *Pace* ONLINE

BUSINESS VOCABULARY

visual aids   charts, graphs, and other images that let audience members use their eyes to process a message

Presenting Ideas and Concepts Visually

Visual aids allow your audience to see your information as well as hear it. However, visual aids help you communicate only if you use them well. Used well, they present more information, emphasize certain points, clarify difficult points, and hold the audience's attention. Used poorly, however, they can confuse people, distract them, and even put them to sleep.

Show and Tell. A good presentation will often include not only words but also images. Images can help you get your message across. Images also can make you look good.

" *There are four ways, and only four ways, in which we have contact with the world. We are evaluated and classified by these four contacts: what we do, how we look, what we say, and how we say it.* **"**

Dale Carnegie,
Author of How to Win Friends and
Influence People

concept ideas that apply to various things or situations and are not necessarily easy to visualize

" *I use many props. The props act as cue cards reminding me of what to say next.* **"**

Tom Ogden,
Writer and Performer

The Visual Presentation

When you speak to an audience, you are depending on words and sounds to deliver your message. Words, of course, are a powerful communication tool, and the expression in the human voice can put even more power in those words. But words often get confusing. Sometimes they refer to concepts and ideas that are hard to visualize. Sometimes a speech delivers information faster than the audience can absorb it. Sometimes your ideas are less than ideally organized. Visual presentations can help fix some of these problems.

When to Use Visual Aids

Visual aids don't always make a presentation better. They must serve a purpose. Some serve to

- Present charts and graphs that show trends, comparisons, and so forth.
- Illustrate abstract **concepts;** that is, ideas that can apply to various things or situations and are not necessarily easy to visualize. "Danger," for example, is a concept. A child dashing into a busy street illustrates that concept.
- Show pictures of things, places, people, and so on.
- Explain and illustrate something complicated or hard to explain, such as a place, product, or process.

Types of Visual Aids

A visual aid is just about anything that an audience can see. What you use will depend on many things, such as your topic or your audience size. Read the examples of visual aids being used today. Think about what you have seen used and how effective it was.

PowerPoint Presentations PowerPoint presentations are images generated by a computer and projected onto a screen. The images are prepared beforehand and stored in a laptop computer. The computer is connected to a projector that projects the images onto a screen. The speaker can proceed through a series of images on individual "slides."

- *Advantages*. PowerPoint presentations are easy to produce on a personal computer. The images, which can include photographs, written words, charts, and graphs, are easily corrected or changed. The series of images also can be printed out on paper for distribution. The presentation can be stored on a disk or sent over the Internet, making it easy to transport. Also, disks can be distributed, making it possible for people to review the presentation later. Finally, the equipment is quiet.
- *Disadvantages*. Software can be hard to learn. Technical problems may be impossible to fix during a presentation. Equipment and software are expensive; presentation depends on equipment available at the site. For best projection, the room must be darkened, which might cause drowsiness.

Slide Shows   Slide shows are a series of photographic slides that project information and images onto a screen. Sophisticated slide shows may involve dozens of projectors and thousands of slides. Slide shows have been largely replaced by PowerPoint presentations.

- *Advantages*. Slide shows offer the highest-quality projection of images. Simple photography can be used to produce slides of images.
- *Disadvantages*. Transportation of slides can be difficult. A specialized company may be needed to produce slides of written words, charts, and graphs. Slides cannot be changed except by making new slides. The technology is relatively simple, but it can still break down. Slide shows demand a darkened room, which may cause drowsiness.

Video Programs   Video Programs presented on a television offer the possibility of sound and moving images. They are very good for demonstrating processes, touring facilities, and showing remote locations.

- *Advantages*. Videotapes are easy to transport and duplicate. They can all but replace the need for an actual speaker.
- *Disadvantages*. Video programs are expensive to produce and all but impossible to change. Tapes cannot be used if a TV is not available. It's hard for a speaker to talk about the program while it's in progress.

Transparency Projections   Transparencies project images drawn on a clear sheet of plastic.

- *Advantages*. It is a quick, inexpensive way to produce basic visual material. It's possible to write on the transparency during the presentation. The technology is simple.
- *Disadvantages*. Images are limited to words and drawings. Projectors can be a little loud. The darkened room may cause drowsiness.

Opaque Projectors   Opaque Projectors can project an image from a book or piece of paper.

- *Advantages*. It is a quick, inexpensive way to project images from paper. It is a simple technology.
- *Disadvantages*. Image is poor. Projector is loud and not widely available. Room must be dark.

Flip Charts   Flip charts are large pads of paper usually set on an easel or hung on a wall. They are used when the speaker needs to write information during a presentation.

- *Advantages.* It is a cheap, easy, foolproof technology. It allows speakers to present information as it is mentioned. It is very useful for audience input. Room can be well lit.
- *Disadvantages.* It is not possible to prepare impressive images (such as charts and photos) beforehand. It is not visible to large audiences. Speaker must write while talking. Information can become jumbled and illegible.

Handouts   Handouts are papers such as explanations, charts, spreadsheets, brochures, and so forth that are distributed to the audience.

- *Advantages.* Audience can take the materials home. It is a cheap, easy technology. It may be reproduced on a copier and may be easy to change (before reproducing).
- *Disadvantages.* Materials, may distract the audience. It can be hard to transport large quantities.

Objects   Also called *props,* objects include products used in demonstrations. It is ideal if the audience can touch and work with the object. You could also bring a *prototype,* an original version of a machine or product. It may or may not be a working model.

- *Advantages.* Props are easy to use in conjunction with other visual aids. Nothing is as effective at showing what the thing looks like, how it works, and so on. They attract attention and can be easily explained and demonstrated.
- *Disadvantages.* Props can be hard to transport. They may not be visible to a large audience. They might break if they are fragile.

Designing Your Message

❝ *No one can remember more than three points.* **❞**

Philip Crosby,
Writer and Consultant
on Quality Management

Visual aids don't necessarily clarify things for your audience. If poorly designed or organized, they can actually distract or confuse your audience. You can avoid such problems by following a few, basic Do's and Don'ts of visual communication.

Do:

- Be silent while the audience reads a projection or handout, then direct attention to yourself. Or read it aloud for your audience, but don't add to it until you read it all.
- Keep written information very short, preferably in list form. (See Figure 3.3.)
- Present just one new idea or fact on each slide, letting sequential slides accumulate into a list.
- Use numbers, bullets, and bold and italic fonts to organize lists.
- Use charts and graphs to help put data in perspective.
- Make handouts available if you are using a projector to present a lot of information.
- Remind the audience that handouts are available.
- Use upper- and lowercase for written words, never all uppercase.
- Arrive early and test equipment before you start. Have a contingency plan in case it fails.
- Speak to your audience, not to your visual aid.

Don't:

- Talk while the audience is reading.
- Present an entire list at one time. First, present the first line. Then present the first and second line, and so on.

Figure 3.3 *Building a List*

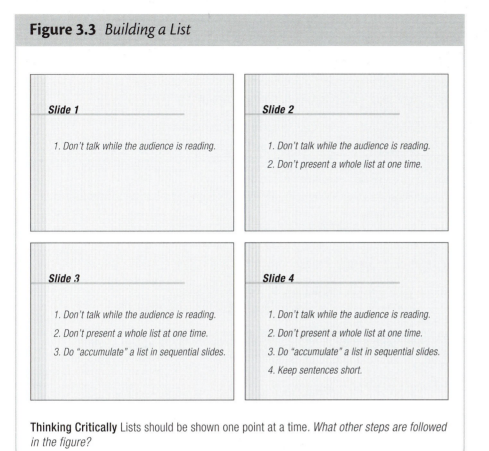

Slide 1

1. Don't talk while the audience is reading.

Slide 2

1. Don't talk while the audience is reading.
2. Don't present a whole list at one time.

Slide 3

1. Don't talk while the audience is reading.
2. Don't present a whole list at one time.
3. Do "accumulate" a list in sequential slides.

Slide 4

1. Don't talk while the audience is reading.
2. Don't present a whole list at one time.
3. Do "accumulate" a list in sequential slides.
4. Keep sentences short.

Thinking Critically Lists should be shown one point at a time. *What other steps are followed in the figure?*

- Leave the room dark for too long, especially after a meal.
- Use a visual aid for the sake of showing off technology. Use it only to help communicate.
- Speak to the visual aid.
- Present the information until the right moment.
- Leave projected information on screen any longer than necessary.

The Audience Perspective

One rule has priority over all others: Do whatever conveys the message best. Analyze your presentation from your audience's point of view. They will want to receive your message (1) bit by bit, (2) in a logical order, (3) without trying to listen and read at the same time, and (4) with constant reminders of what they've just learned and what they'll learn next.

Word Pictures

If nothing else, consider adding "word pictures" to your speech. Word pictures help your audience see something in their minds when you can't use an actual visual aid. Instead of saying that your new rice steamer does all the work for you, call it your live-in chef. Or instead of saying that your new program eliminates all those pop-up ads, call it your gatekeeper, guarding your screen from those nasty little pop-ups.

PRESENTING IDEAS AND CONCEPTS VISUALLY

- Good visual aids help communicate, but poor ones can confuse and distract.
- Visual aids should be used for a purpose, such as illustrating a concept or a complicated subject.
- Each type of visual aid has advantages and disadvantages.
- Objects (props) are an excellent way to illustrate and demonstrate, and they help hold an audience's attention.
- Visual aids should present information in small measures.

CHECK YOURSELF

1. List four good purposes of visual aids.
2. When can a flip chart be more effective than a PowerPoint presentation?

Check your answers online at www.mhhe.com/pace.

BUSINESS VOCABULARY

concept   ideas that apply to various things or situations and are not necessarily easy to visualize

Chapter Summary

3.1 Communicating in Writing

Objective: Write more clearly and logically in the language and formats of business.

In this section, you learned about the nature and power of words. Words can be used most effectively if the writer first thinks about the purpose of the words, the message to be conveyed, and the information needed for the message. While writing, the writer should try for simplicity, clarity, and organization. Revision is an essential last step. This section also described a few forms of writing, such as e-mail, letters, and reports.

3.2 Thinking Critically and Creatively

Objective: Solve problems by thinking critically and creatively.

In this section, you considered two different approaches to problem solving: one critical, the other creative. Critical thinking applies logic and a methodical use of facts and data from which a hypothesis is developed. Creative thinking puts logic and preformulated ideas aside to look for solutions in situations that are different but in some way similar. Used together, critical and creative thinking are a powerful means of solving problems.

3.3 Developing Your Vocabulary

Objective: Expand your vocabulary by using a dictionary and understanding the principles behind words.

In this section, you saw how business language uses various kinds of words to convey ideas in a business context.

Recognizing that words are a powerful tool, you studied a few ways to expand your vocabulary. You also learned that understanding the parts of words, will help you to learn new words with those same parts. You also learned how to use a dictionary to find not only spelling and definitions but also the usage and roots of words.

3.4 Making Speeches and Presentations

Objective: Effectively and confidently present in formation to an audience.

In this section, you saw that public speaking and presentations are excellent opportunities to further your career. By preparing, you can put your fears behind you. Preparation involves knowing your audience, gathering your facts, writing what you're going to say, and rehearsing it until you're comfortable with every line. You also studied some of the characteristics of a good speech and some of the techniques for good delivery.

3.5 Presenting Ideas and Concepts Visually

Objective: Use visual aids and graphic explanations to present ideas and concepts.

In this section, you examined the power of appropriately designed visual aids. Each kind of visual aid has its advantages and disadvantages. You read useful tips that will help you convey your message while avoiding confusion and distraction.

Business Vocabulary

- acronyms (p. 82)
- brainstorm (p. 79)
- bullet (p. 72)
- communication media (p. 70)
- concept (p. 92)
- creative thinking (p. 77)
- critical thinking (p. 77)
- euphemisms (p. 82)
- format (p. 72)
- hypothesis (p. 78)
- jargon (p. 82)
- letterhead (p. 72)
- memorandum (or memo) (p. 72)
- netiquette (p. 75)
- slang (p. 83)
- stereotype (p. 78)
- subheads (p. 72)
- technical words (p. 82)
- trade publications (p. 83)
- visual aids (p. 86)
- vogue words (p. 82)
- vulgarity (p. 83)

Key Concept Review

1. List five differences between written words and spoken words. (3.1)

2. Name three things you should think about before you start a writing project. (3.1)

3. Name the two approaches to solving a problem. (3.2)

4. List five ways to avoid obstacles to creative thinking. (3.2)

5. Name three sources of new words for your vocabulary. (3.3)

6. What can you learn from a dictionary besides spelling and meaning? (3.3)

7. Why should you not pass up an opportunity to give a speech or make a presentation? (3.4)

8. What are the five steps of preparation for a speech or presentation, and how do they help conquer stage fright? (3.4)

9. List four good reasons to use visual aids. (3.5)

10. What are the advantages and disadvantages of using PowerPoint for a presentation? (3.5)

Online Project

Use the Internet to quickly learn some of the jargon and technical language that is used in your desired professional field. A search engine will help you find the annual reports of related companies and organizations, articles about your field, laws and regulations, and so on. Try to use each Web site to get an idea of other Web sites to visit. List 25 words that you might be able to use in your résumé.

Step Up the *Pace*

CASE A   *Revising a Report*

Your team has worked long and hard to write a lengthy report on changes that need to be made to your company's manufacturing process. You've put together a huge amount of information about equipment, costs, new technology, computer applications, training, rates of output, projected revenues, and possible new products. Your boss says it's a great collection of information but a lousy report. It's confusing, boring, and way too long.

What to Do

1. Write an outline for your report, including a few subtopics for each section.
2. How would you change this information to make it easier to understand, less boring, and shorter?

CASE B   *Sales Presentation*

You were excited about being made a regional sales manager until you learned that the job involves sales presentations to potential new customers. You're nervous about speaking before a group, but you know it's important to your career. Your product is a complicated one, involving computer hardware, specialized software, Internet connections, a leasing package, a training program, and ongoing maintenance. You have to give your sales presentation in three different cities.

What to Do

1. Write an outline of your presentation. It should cover not just the features of the product but also such issues as cost, installation, uses for the customer's manufacturing process, and benefits. In your outline, include the kinds of visual aids you will use and the kinds of information you will present visually.
2. Explain how you use a flip chart as you discuss the customer's needs. What questions would you ask? What would you write on the flip chart?

Create a Professional Outgoing Message

As a busy professional you need a to have an efficient message-taking system. The message callers hear on your extension or cell phone should both help them and reflect your professionalism. Follow these tips when creating an outgoing message:

- Say your name clearly so callers know they have called the correct number.
- Be brief. Don't go into lengthy explanations of why you're not available.
- Say what information you need, such as how to get back to the caller. If you get frequent calls about problems with orders, ask for information to help you be prepared, such as an invoice number. Then, you can find the invoice before you call them back.
- Don't ask for too much information. Two or three things is all your caller will be able to remember.
- Write out what you want to say and practice it. Then, listen to your recorded message. If you don't like it, do it over!
- Vary your pitch as you speak; don't speak in a monotone.
- If there are other options for the caller, such as returning to the main menu, tell the caller how.
- Everyone knows about the beep by now. However, if there is no beep or there's a long pause before the beep, warn callers about that.
- Call your own line to hear your message and to make sure the options work as expected.
- Get in the habit of checking your messages when you return to your desk.
- Remember to call people back within 24 hours of their call.

Which message sounds the most professional?

A. Hi, this is Terry Mack. I must be at lunch or in a meeting. So, leave a message at the beep, and I'll get back to you as soon as I can!

B. Thanks for calling Terry Mack. Please leave a brief message. If this is a driver, please give your PSS number and your dispatcher.

C. This is Terry Mack. Please leave me a brief message. If this is a delivery driver, please give your PSS number, your route, your current location, and your dispatcher. I will get back to you as soon as I can. To return to the main menu, press zero, then star. Thanks!

Option B will prompt the caller to leave the most useful information.

Exercise: Write out your own message, practice it, then record it on your office or cell phone. Remember to check it once you finish!

_____
_____
_____
_____
_____
_____
_____
_____

Glossary

A

acronyms words formed by the first letters in a phrase, such as ROM in CD-ROM

aptitude a natural ability to either do certain things or learn to do them, such as an aptitude for math or for working with others

assets things that have value, such as a house, stocks and bonds, and a car

B

bankruptcy the legal situation in which you admit that you cannot pay all of your debts on time

benchmark skills the big skills that you definitely need for your career

benchmarks points or standards from which you can measure or locate other things; in terms of goals, the important goals that are unlikely to change

bond a company's or government's promise to pay back a sum of money plus interest over time

brainstorm a group process of tossing out ideas and looking for ways that one of them might actually work

budget a set amount of money to spend on different categories of expenses

bullet a dot marking an item in a list

business loan a loan to start or expand a business

C

career goals goals that should move you forward in your professional development

cash flow projection an estimate of how much you will earn and how much you will spend

communication media means of relating information

concept ideas that apply to various things or situations and are not necessarily easy to visualize

contingency an alternate plan to be used if things go wrong

creative thinking an intuitive, nonlogical approach to solving a problem by being open to inspiration from unexpected sources

critical thinking a logical, analytical, methodical approach to understanding a problem and working toward a solution

D

delegating assigning a project, responsibility, or authority to someone else

E

effectiveness the extent to which efforts produce expected results

efficiency the ratio of input to output; that is, the amount of energy that is put into the production of something compared to the quantity actually produced

euphemisms relatively soft words that replace harsher words

F

finance the science of managing money and other assets

format the standard form and structure of formal written communication

G

goals the ultimate aim of your efforts

H

home equity loan a loan secured by the value of your house

hypothesis a possible but unproven solution

I

income tax a tax based on a percentage of money earned

J

jargon words that are used in specific fields and trades

job goals goals that assure you and management that you are doing your job well

L

lateral shifts shifts that move you over to a new kind of job rather than up the corporate ladder

letterhead letter paper printed with the name, address, and logo of the company in a unique format and color

M

memorandum (or memo) official written message from one individual to another individual or to a group, usually within the same company

mentor a professional who is willing to guide you through your job and teach you about the business

multitasking the activity of working on more than one task at a time

mutual fund a portfolio of both stock and bond investments

N

netiquette good manners for communicating by e-mail

network to put yourself in places where you might meet people who may help you

P

patterns of behavior things you tend to do fairly regularly, things that might be called habits

portfolio a set of investments

prioritize put things in order of importance; rate the importance of a task

procrastination the act of putting off until later what you should do now

R

résumé a summary of your education, training, skills, and professional experience

revenues all your income, including tips, commissions, gifts of money, and interest

S

skill resources a list of places where you might go to learn new skills

skills a specific thing you have learned how to do

skills inventory a categorized list of things you can do, could do, and would like to do

slang informal language that is considered correct but acceptable only in informal situations

stereotype a mistaken impression that a person shares all the characteristics of similar people

stock rights to having partial ownership of a company

stress an uncomfortable and disruptive mental or emotional state brought on by an outside influence

subheads short subject titles

subsidiaries other companies that your company owns

T

technical words words that are used in specific fields and trades that are strictly technical in nature, especially scientific words

trade publications magazines and newspapers that deal exclusively with a given business or industry

transferable skills skills that you can carry from one job to another, even from one profession to another, such as writing, languages, and so forth

transition a change from one stage of development to another

V

value system the total of all your values and the way they work together

values the basic beliefs that are important to you, the ones that guide your choices and tell you what is right or wrong

visual aids charts, graphs, and other images that let audience members use their eyes to process your message

vogue words words that come into style, often replacing other perfectly correct words

vulgarity offensive and "dirty" words, including the offensive words sometimes used for people of certain nationalities, religions, races, and other groupings

Photo Credits

Index